FANTASTIC, AMAZING AND BEAUTIFUL DIME NOVEL ART

compiled by Joseph A. Lovece

DIME NOVEL COVER SPECIAL EDITION

http://www.steamman.net
joe@steamman.net
https://www.facebook.com/thesteamman

ISBN-13: 978-1508490715
ISBN-10: 1508490716

Also by the author:

The Steam Man of the West
The Road Home
The Flying Prairie Schooner
The Transatlantic Race

Dime Novel Cover:

Denver Doll the Detective Queen
Six Weeks in the Moon
Hank Hound, the Crescent City Detective
Sherlock Holmes Versus Jack the Ripper
Hercules, the Dumb Destroyer
Night Hawk
Sexton Blake: The Missing Millionaire
Lord Lister, known as Raffles, Master Thief
The Witch Hunter's Wards

Introduction

Whether you know it or not we are surrounded by dime novels. It's no coincidence that modern comic books look like magazines over a hundred years old. And likewise Hollywood would not exist without dipping into this pool constantly for imagination, action and adventure, heroes and villains. We still remember some of the names, like Nick Carter and Buffalo Bill, although Fred Fearnot, Diamond Dick, Jr., Ted Strong and Young Wild West have largely escaped from the public's attention.

Key to their popularity was the cover art. They ranged from the mundane to the utterly fantastic: devils, monsters, ghosts, goblins, skeletons, magicians, airships, submarines and mad scientists.

Unlike the authors these unsung artists remain mostly unresearched. At the very least there should be a celebration of the art if not the men.

We know some of their names, although they generally did not sign their work. At publisher Beadle and Adams: G.H. Gouter, Henry Stephens, Arthur Lumley and John R. Chapin. For Frank Tousey and such titles as *Pluck and Luck* and *Work and Win*: Thomas Worth and A. Berghaus. And over at Street and Smith and titles like *Buffalo Bill Stories, Nick Carter Weekly, Diamond Dick Jr. Best Boy Stories* and *Rough Riders Weekly* were Charles L. Wrenn, F.A. Carter and Robert Emmett Owen.

Heroes all.

It was not the intention to provide comprehensive bibliographic information on the examples presented, nor try to penetrate the turgid mist of house pen names (i.e. by The Author of "Buffalo Bill") since many writers may have penned the actual issues involved. Generally the pen name is preserved for the accompanying text.

Buffalo Bill Stories, No. 299, February 2, 1907.
Buffalo Bill's Desperate Dozen; or, The Raiders of
Round Robin Ranch by The Author of "Buffalo Bill"

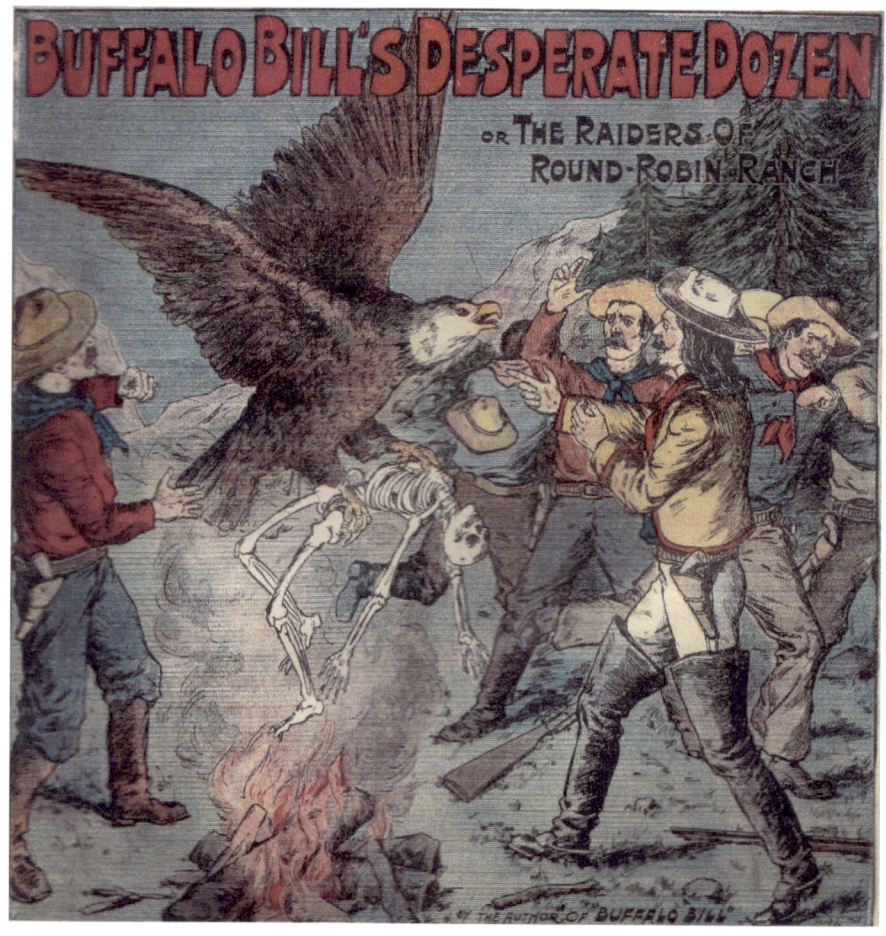

Pluck and Luck No. 963, November 15, 1916. Lost in the Ice by Howard Austin.

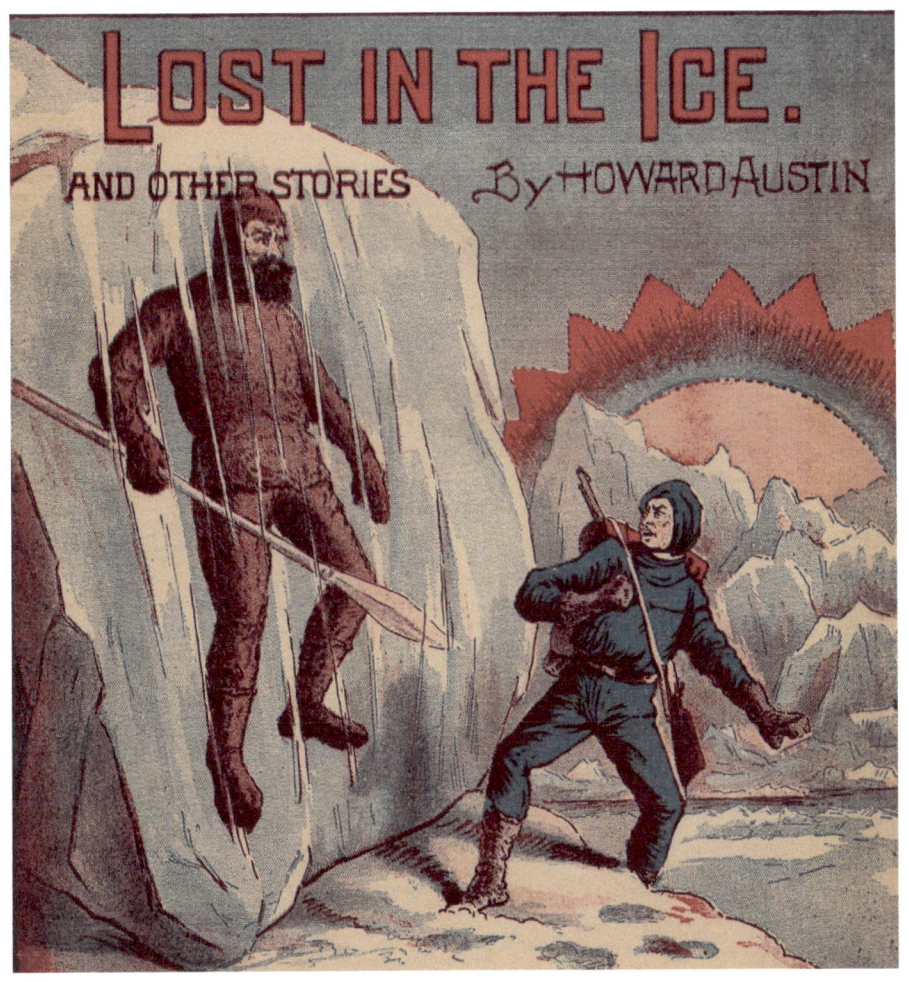

Beadle's Frontier Series No. 36, 1908, The Chief of the Miami; or, the Hand of Fire by Arthur L. Meserve (spelled Messerve on the cover) (1838-1896) and he also wrote for *Golden Argosy, The Fireside Companion, Starr's American Novels* and *Boys' Library*. His pen names included Saco and Duke Cuyler.

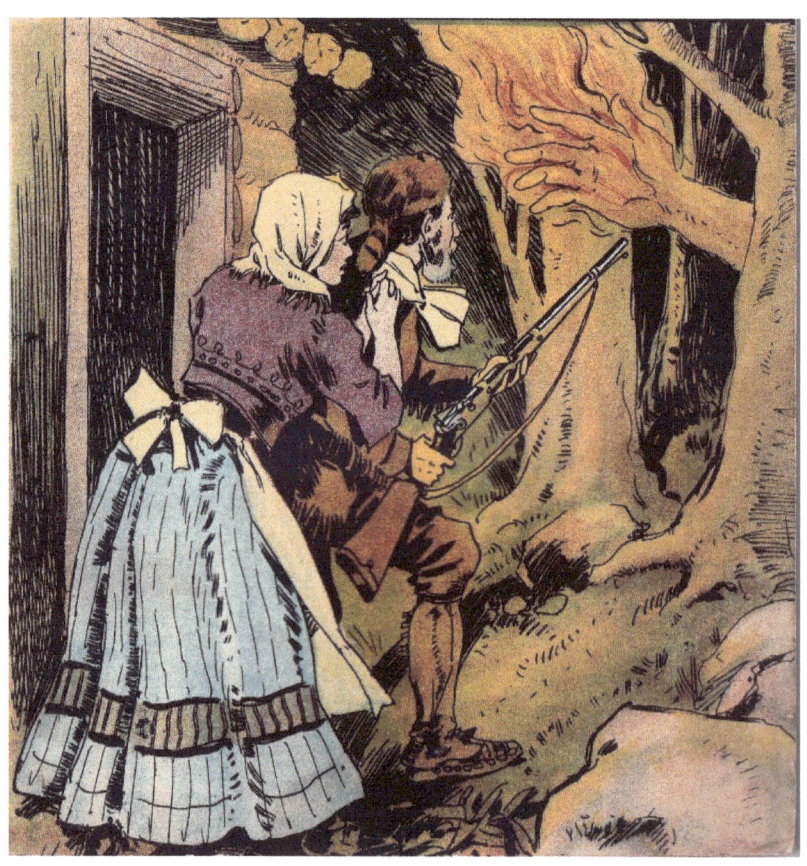

Work and Win No. 157, December 6, 1901, Fred Fearnot and the Medium; or, Having Fun with the "Spirits" by Hal Standish (H. K. Shackleford).

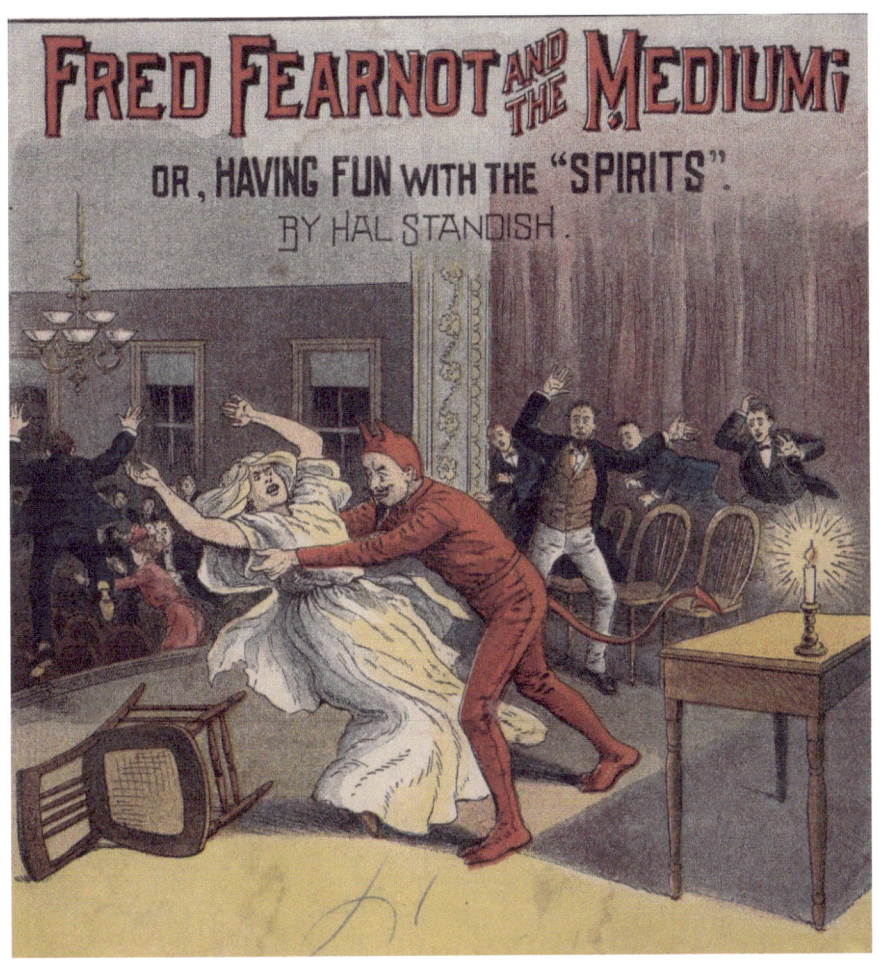

Pluck and Luck No. 897, August 11, 1915. The Rocket; or, Adventures in the Air by Allyn Draper (St. G. Rathbone). Reprinted from a *Young Men of America* serial, beginning in May 1882, as by John Sherman (pen name).

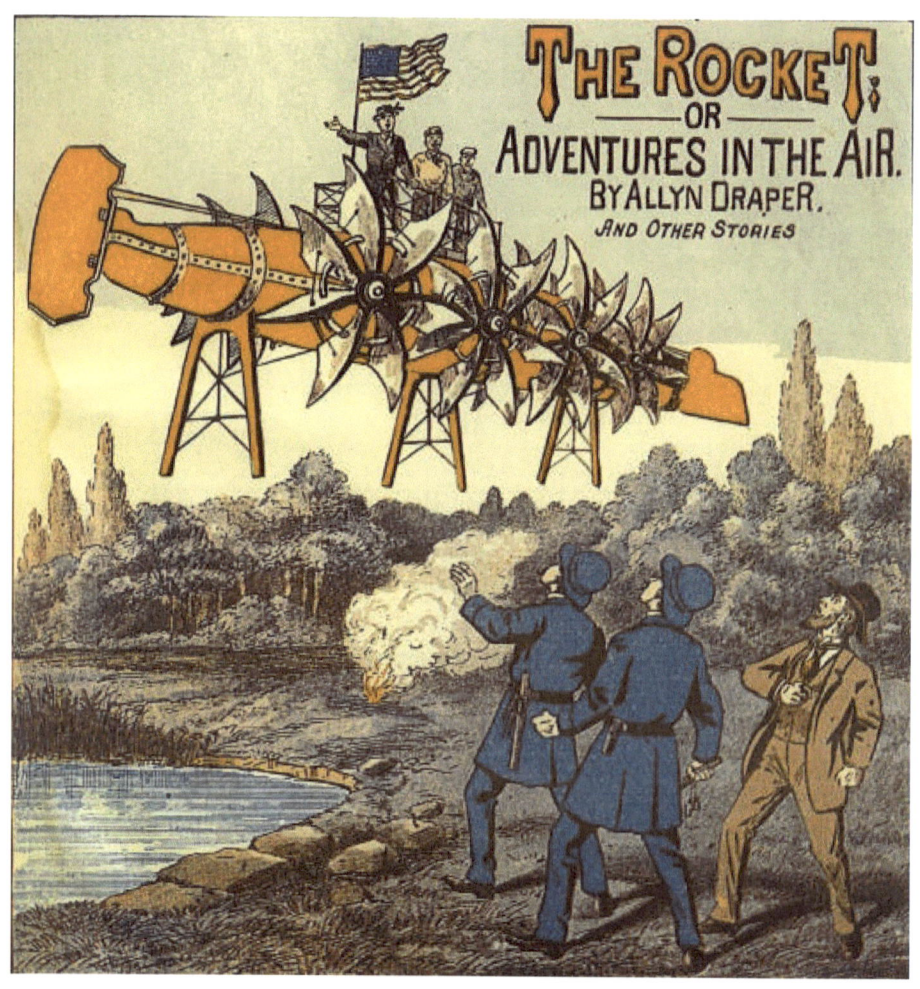

Pluck and Luck No. 401, February 7, 1906. Jack the Juggler; or, A Boy's Search for his Sister by H.K. Shackleford.

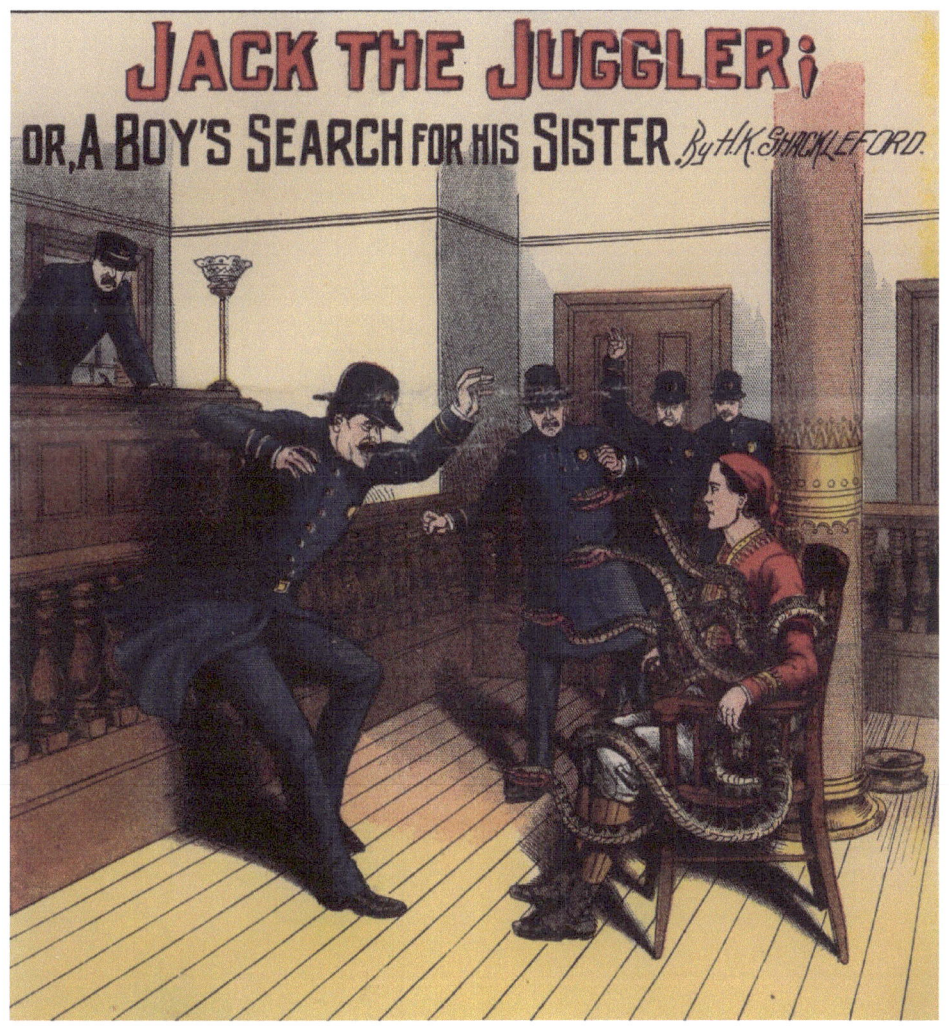

Beadle's Frontier Series No. 35, 1908. The Woman Trapper; or, Arkansas Sal and the Apaches by Col. Prentiss Ingraham. Best known for his Buffalo Bill stories, Ingraham (1843-1904) was a soldier for the confederacy, and was an officer in the Cuban military.

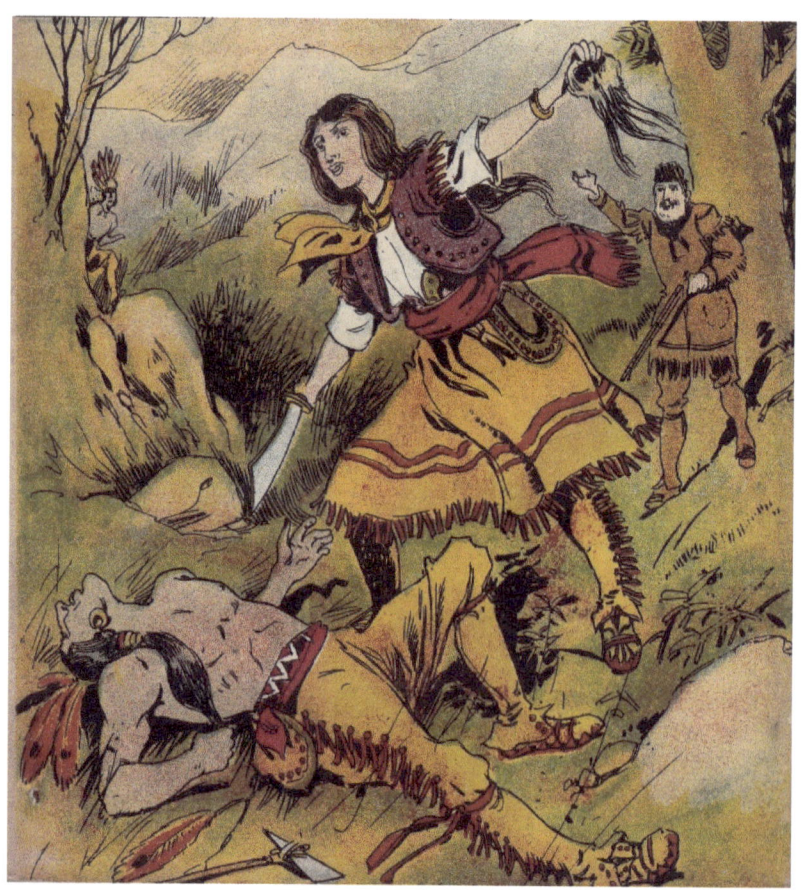

Pluck and Luck No. 917, December 29, 1915. In the Ice, A Story of the Arctic Regions by Howard Austin.

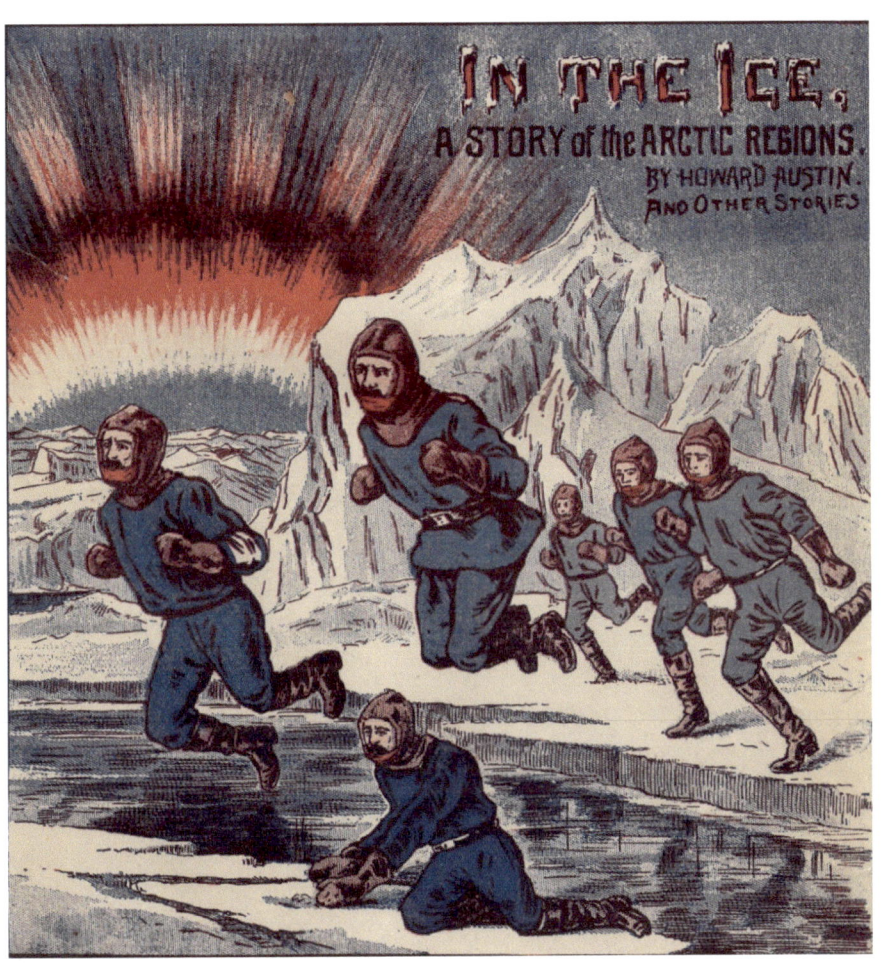

Pluck and Luck No. 74, November 1, 1899, Frank Fair in Congress; or, A Boy among Our Law Makers. A Thrilling Story of Washington by Hal Standsh.

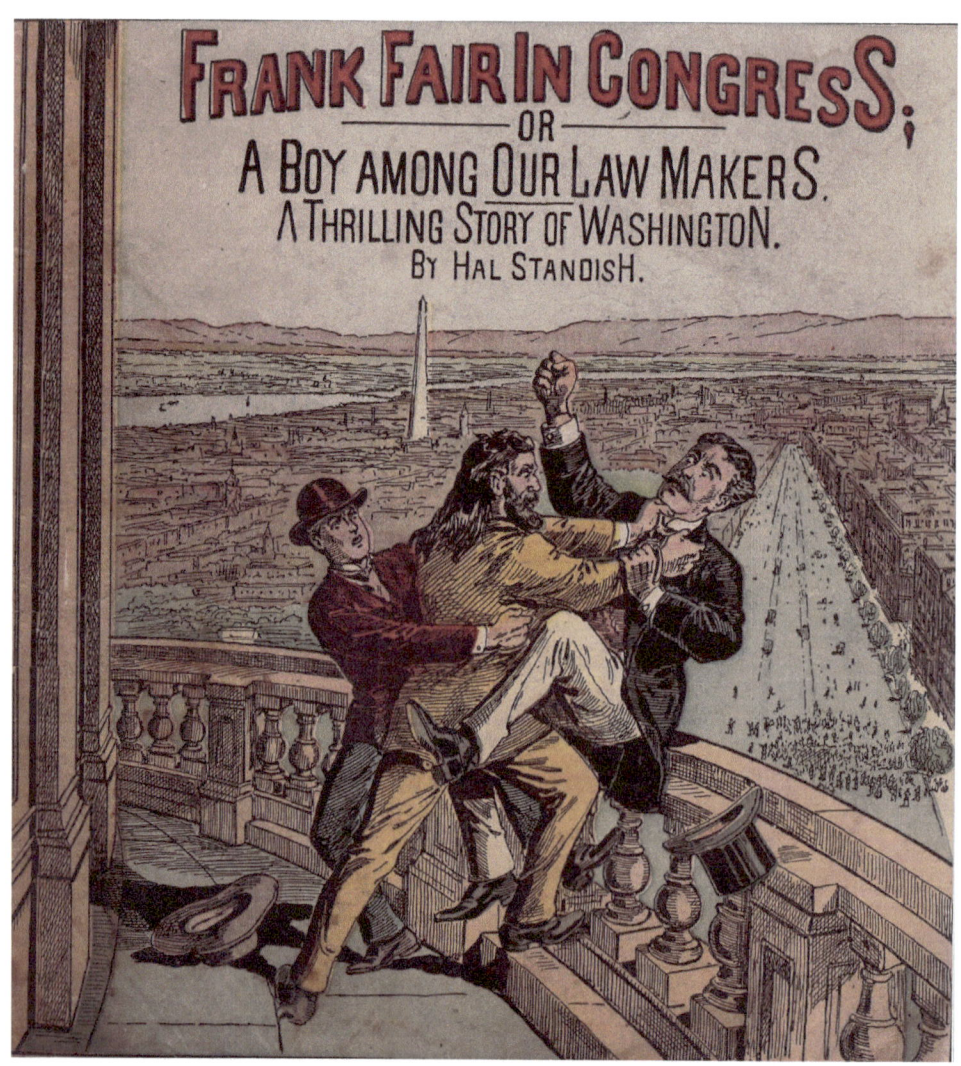

Rough Rider Weekly No. 115, December 15, 1906. King of the Wild West's Danger; or Stella among the Hopis by Ned Taylor, house name for several authors writing the Ted Strong series.

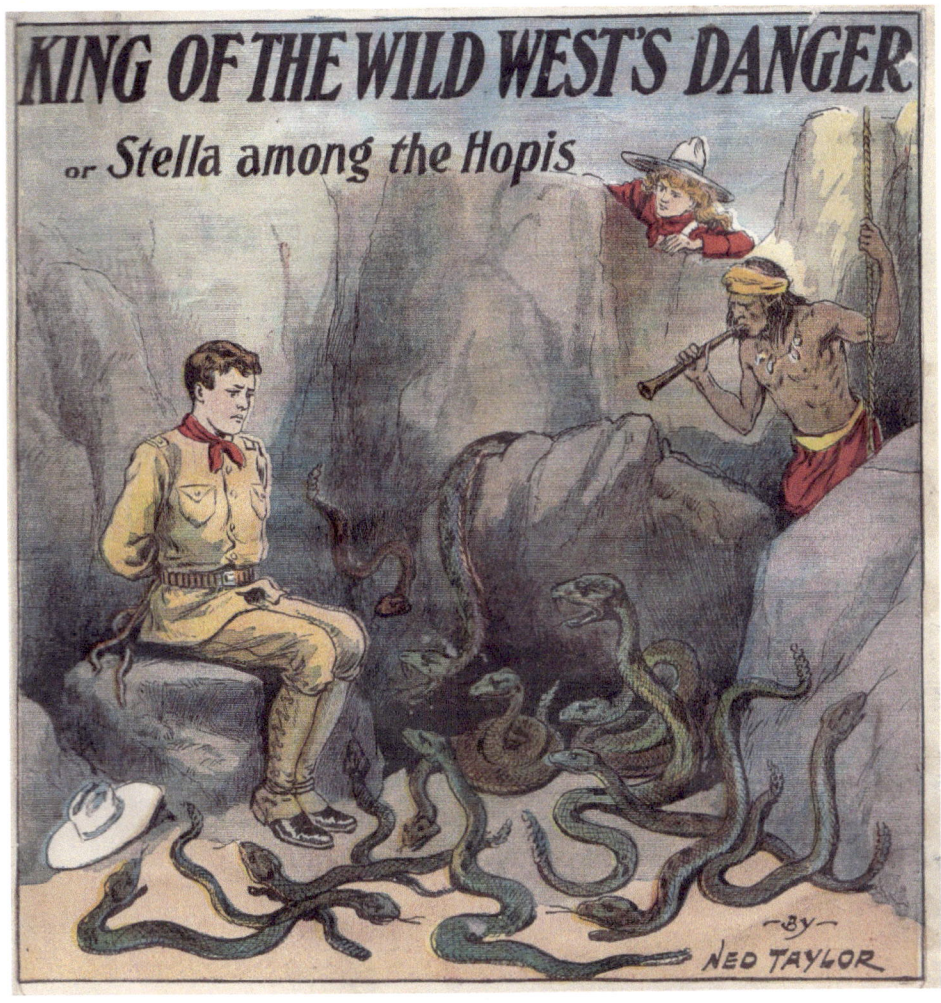

Frank Leslie's Boy's and Girl's Weekly Vol. XIV No. 359, September 6, 1873. Jack Harkaway among the Brigands, anonymous (Bracebridge Hemyng).

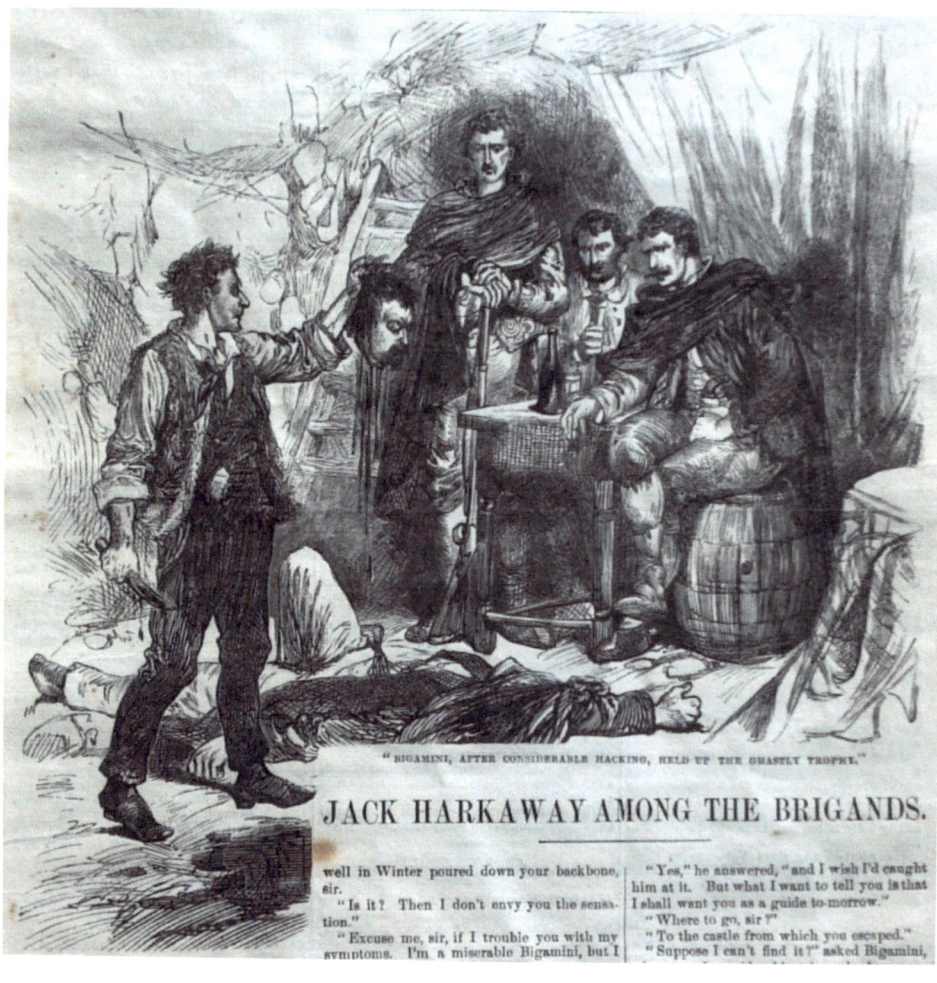

"BIGAMINI, AFTER CONSIDERABLE HACKING, HELD UP THE GHASTLY TROPHY."

JACK HARKAWAY AMONG THE BRIGANDS.

well in Winter poured down your backbone, sir.

"Is it? Then I don't envy you the sensation."

"Excuse me, sir, if I trouble you with my symptoms. I'm a miserable Bigamini, but I

"Yes," he answered, "and I wish I'd caught him at it. But what I want to tell you is that I shall want you as a guide to-morrow."

"Where to go, sir?"

"To the castle from which you escaped."

"Suppose I can't find it?" asked Bigamini,

Motor Stories No. 24, September 30, 1909, Motor Matt's Mandarin; or, Turning a Trick for Tsan Ti by "The Author of Motor Matt" (William Wallace Cook).

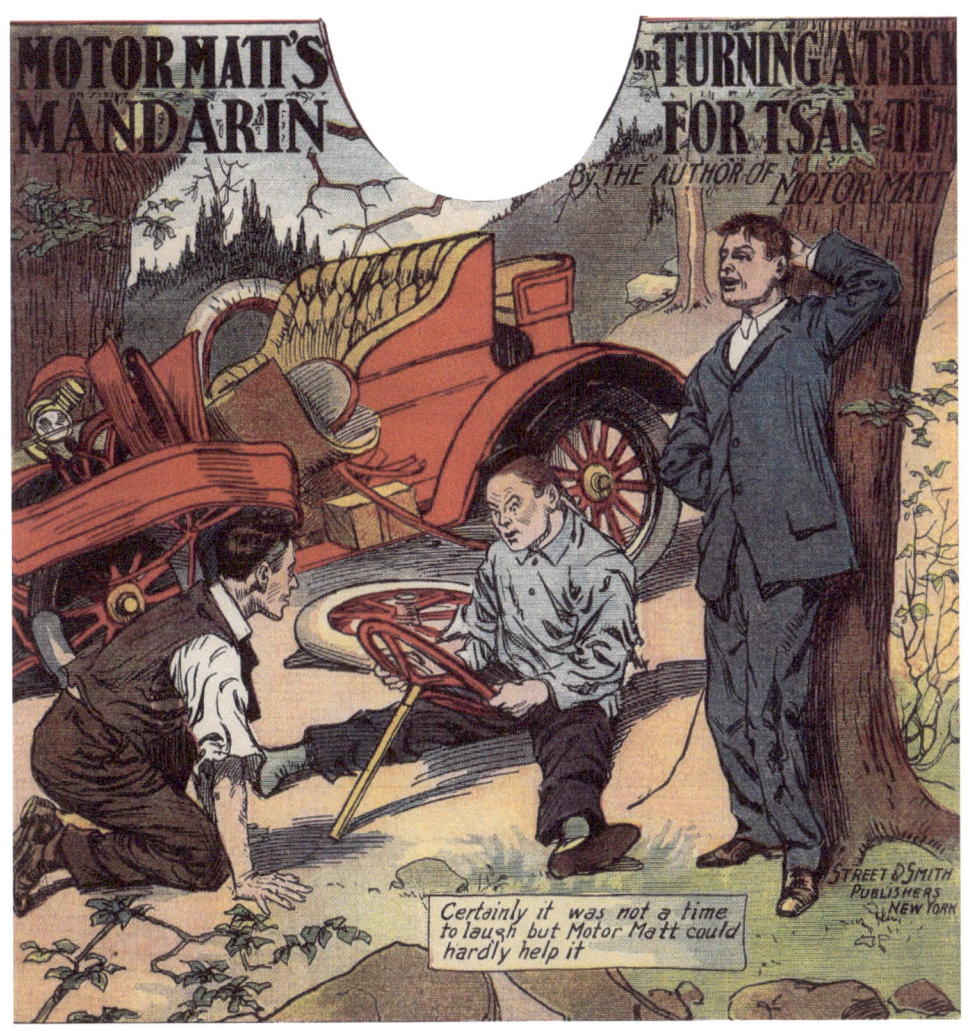

Certainly it was not a time to laugh but Motor Matt could hardly help it

Buffalo Bill Stories No. 289, November 24, 1906,
Buffalo Bill and the Creeping Terror; or, The Black
Spider of the Shoshones by The Author of Buffalo Bill.
At least 13 writers contributed to the series.
Reprinted in *New Buffalo Bill Weekly* No. 88, May 16,
1914; and in Britain in *Wild West Library* No. 188,
1908.

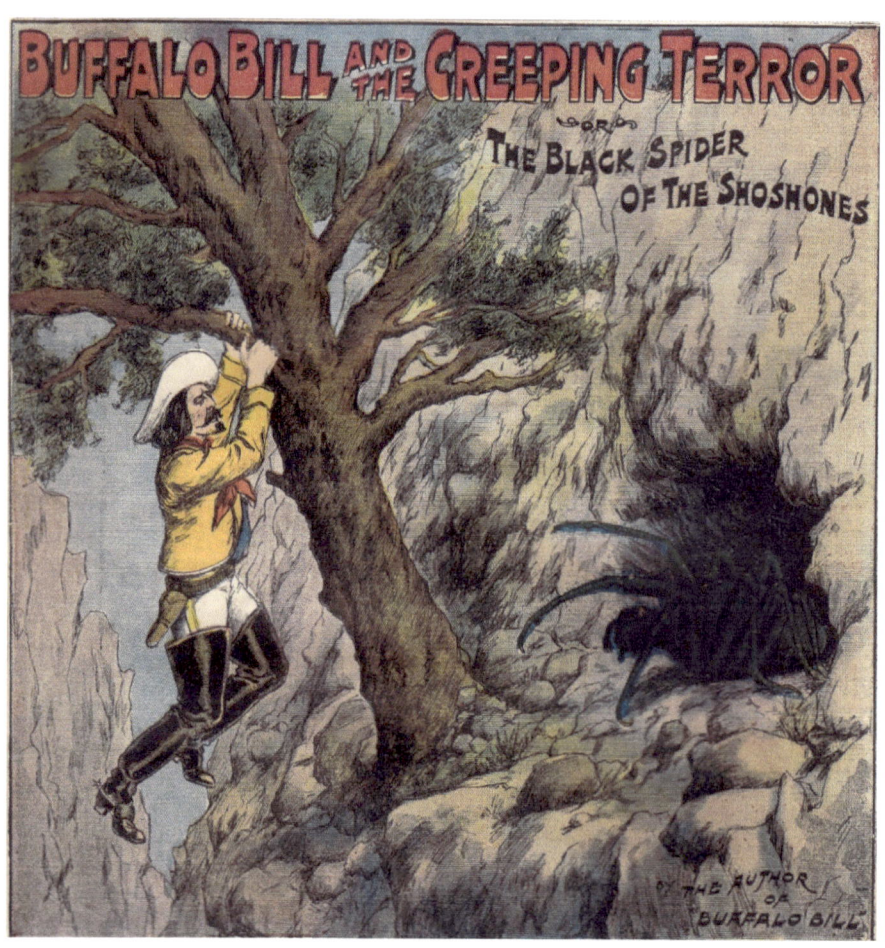

New Nick Carter Weekly No. 565, October 26, 1907. Secrets of a Haunted House edited by Chickering Carter (probably Frederick Van Rensselaer Dey).

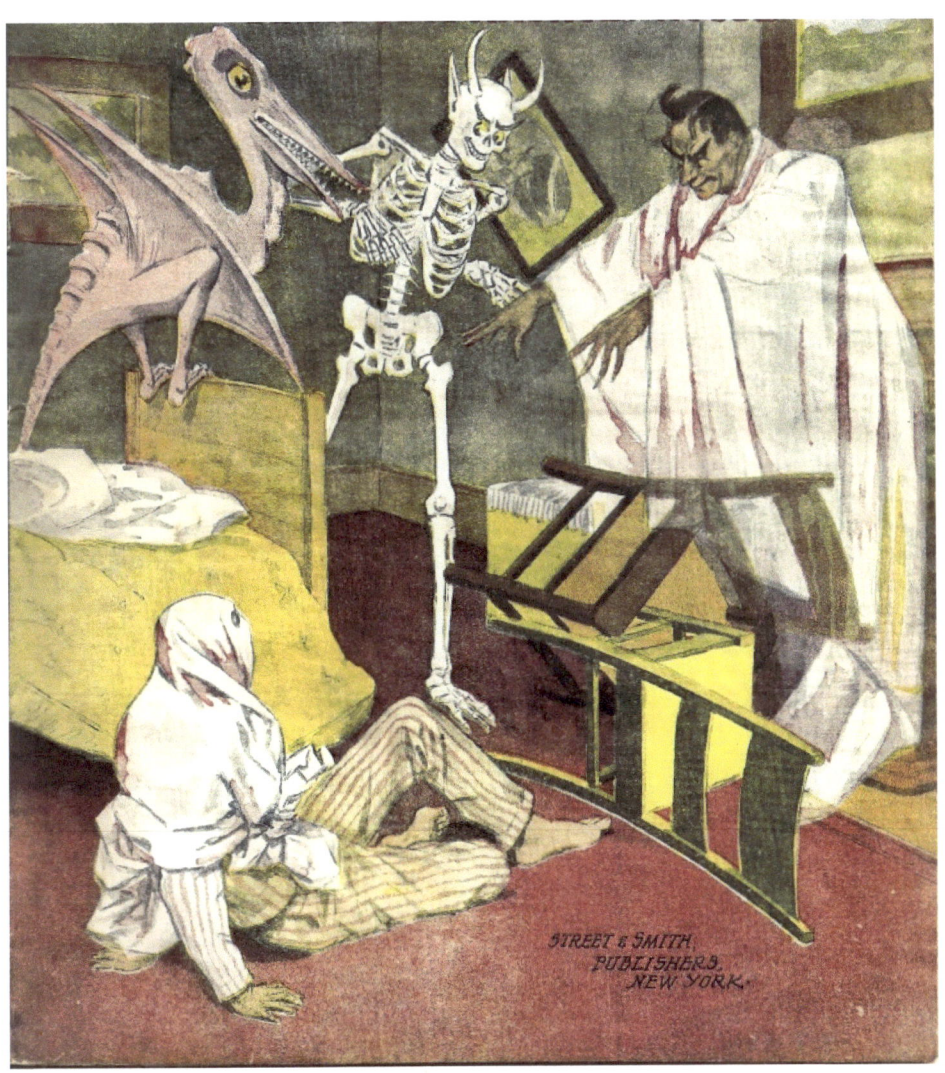

Rough Rider Weekly No. 117, December 29, 1906.
King of the Wild's West's Motor Car; or, Stella
Fosdick's Peril by Ned Taylor.

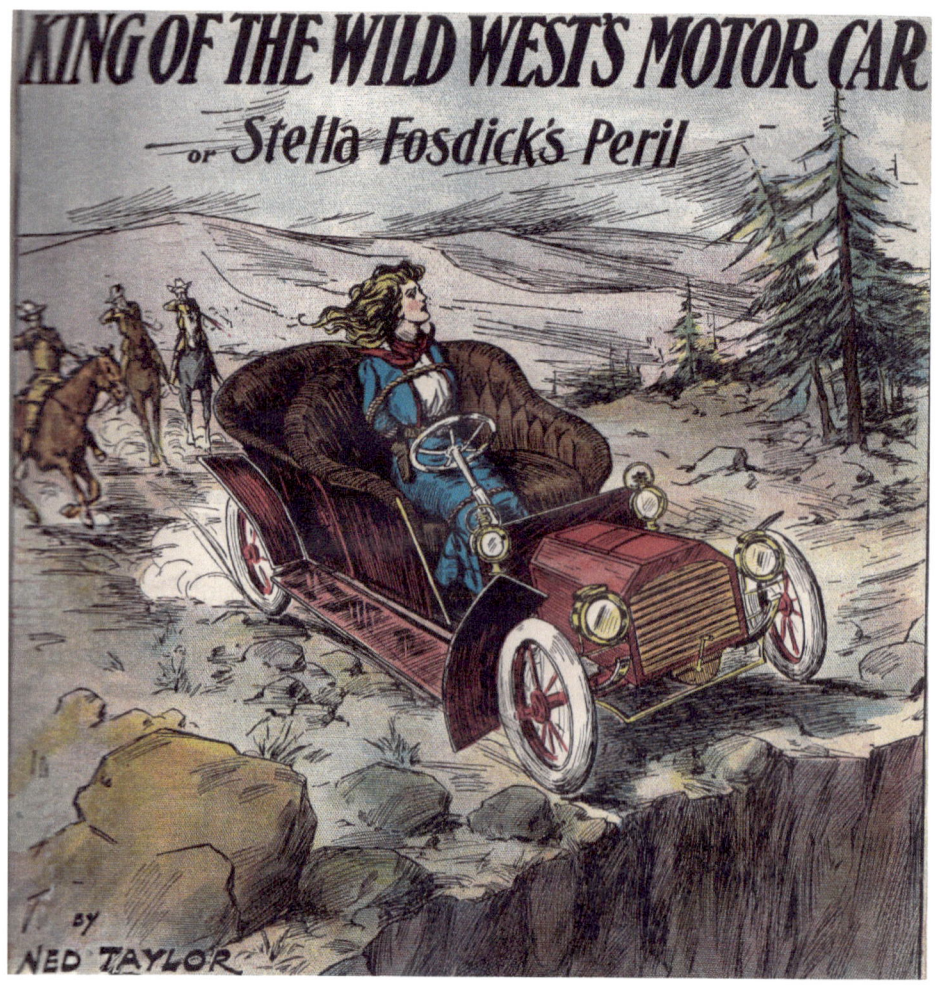

Wild West Weekly No. 255, September 6, 1907.
Young Wild West at Lonesome Licks; or, The
Phantom of Pilgrim's Pass by An Old Scout.

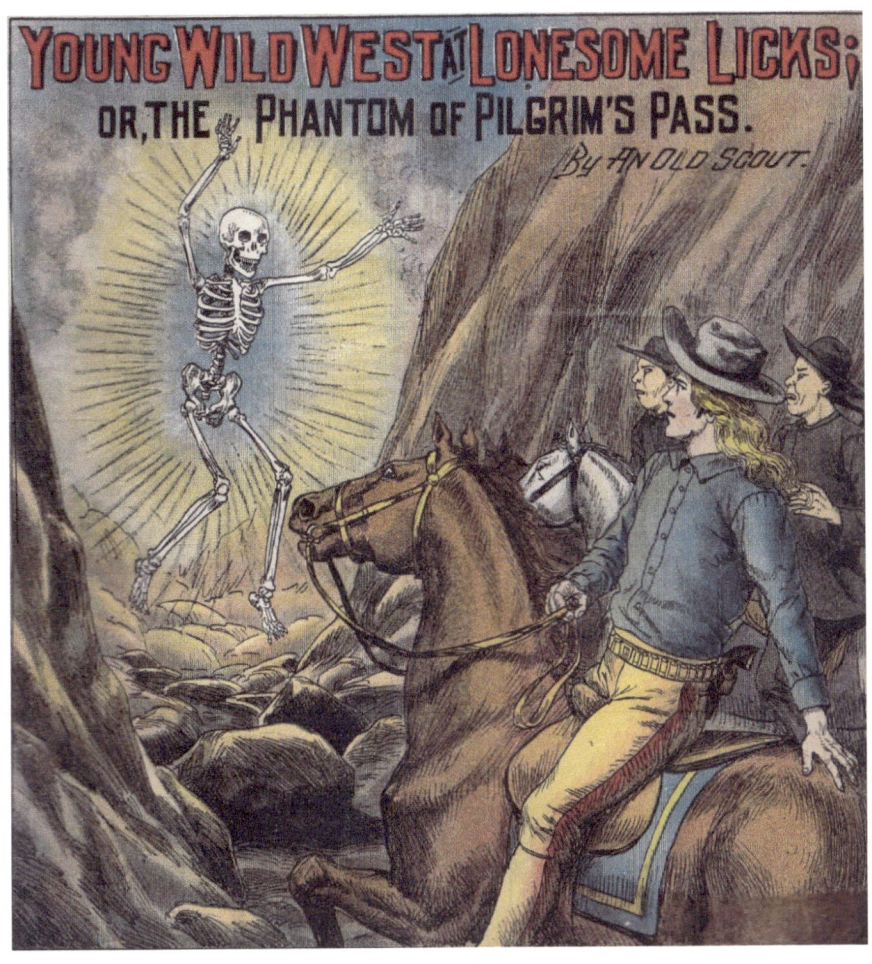

Pluck and Luck No. 258, May 18, 1903. Jack Wright's Demon of the Plains; or, Wild Adventures Among the Cowboys by "Noname" (Luis Senarens).

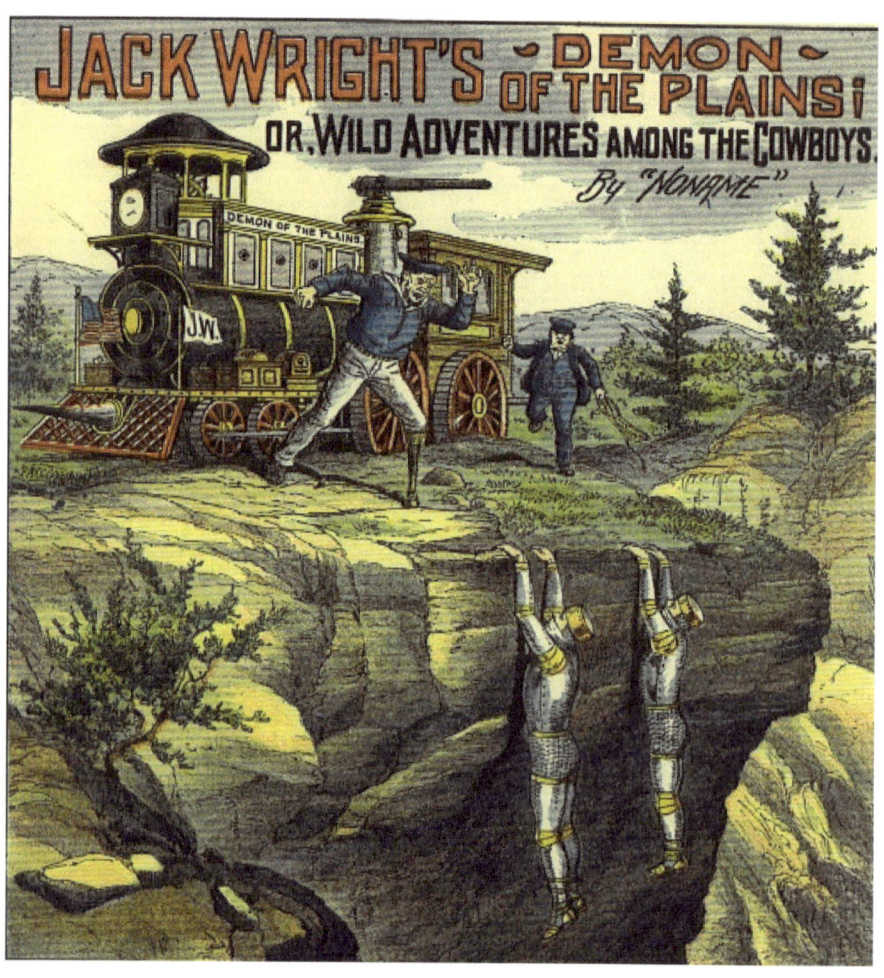

Work and Win No. 941, December 15, 1916. Fred Fearnot and the "Blind Tigers"; or, More Ways than One by Hal Standish.

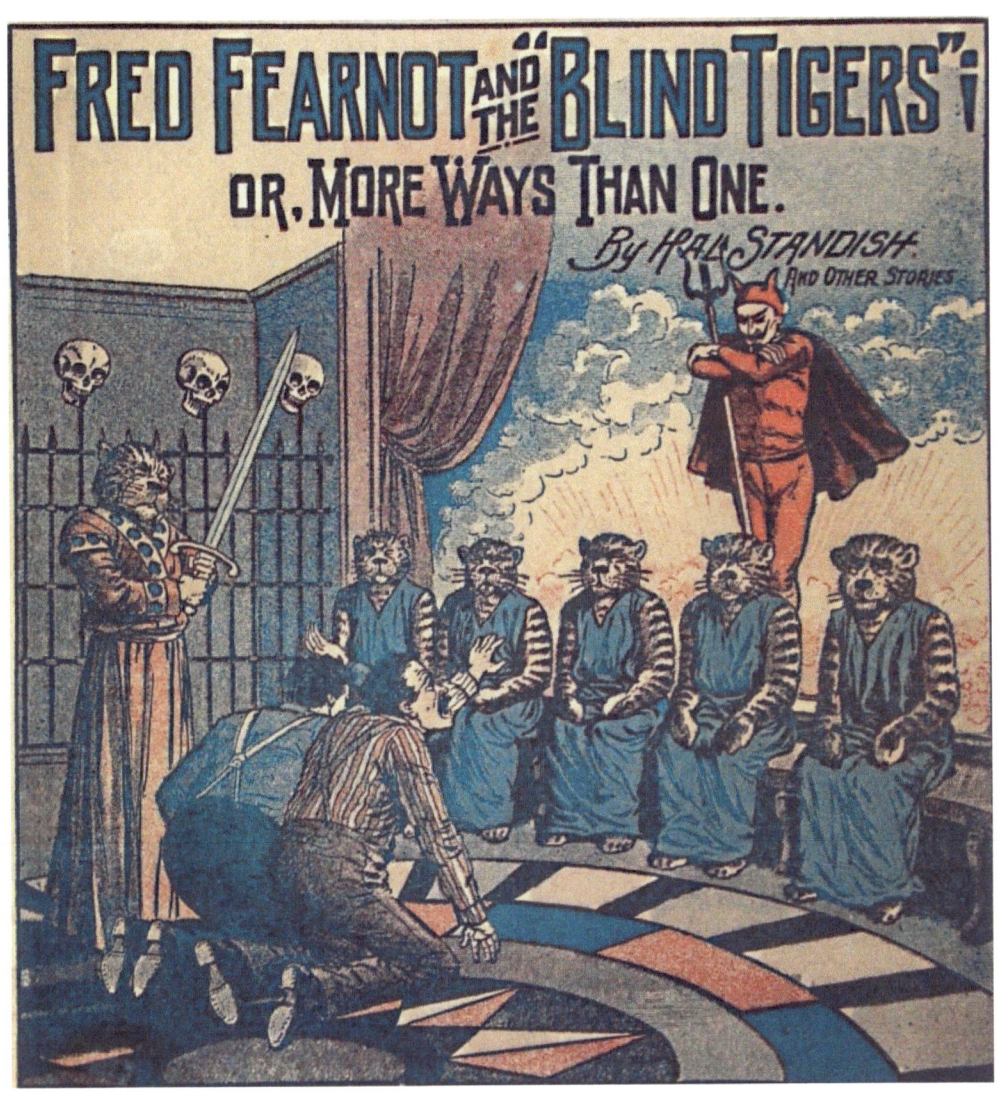

Fame and Fortune Weekly Stories of Boys Who Make Money No. 661, May 31, 1918. A Runaway Boy; or, The Buried Treasures of the Incas by A Self-Made Man, (James Perkins Tracy)..

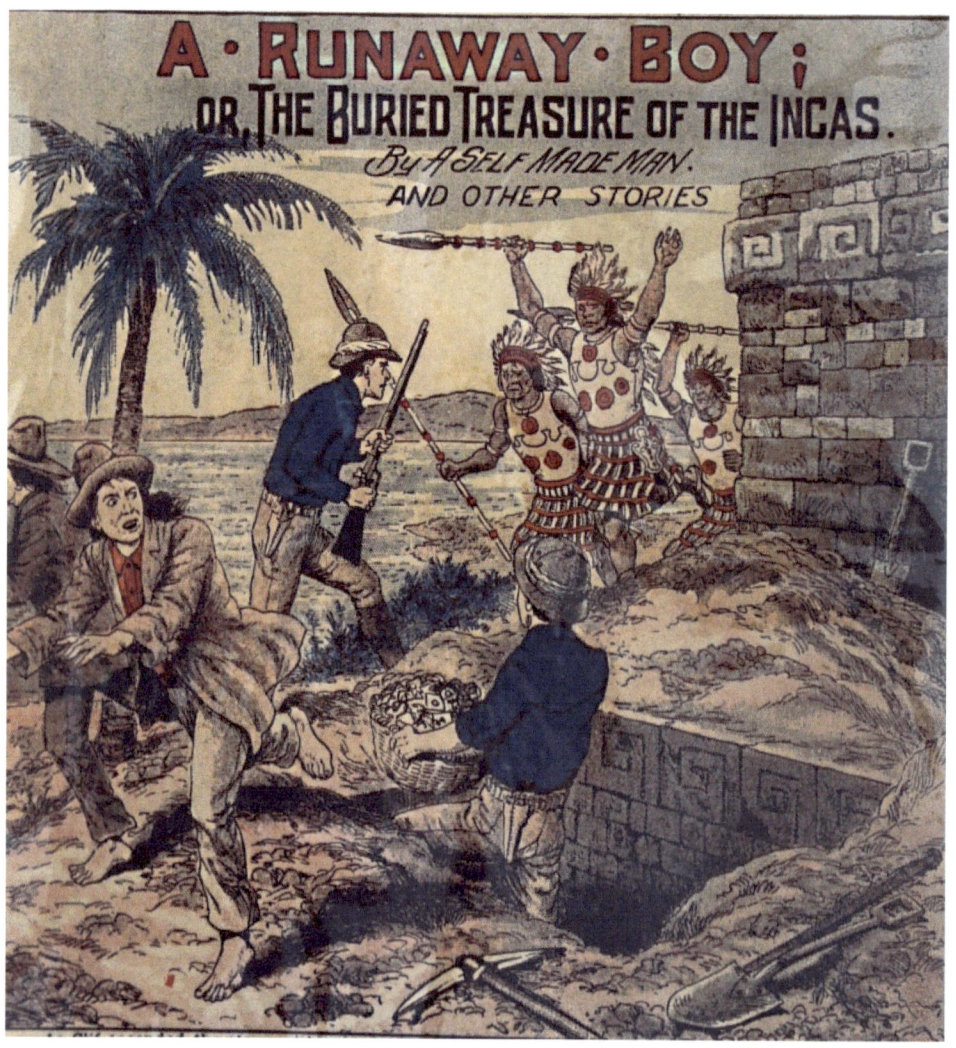

Pluck and Luck 88No. 367, June 14, 1905, The Boy
With the Steel Mask; or, A Face That Was Never Seen
by Allan Arnold.

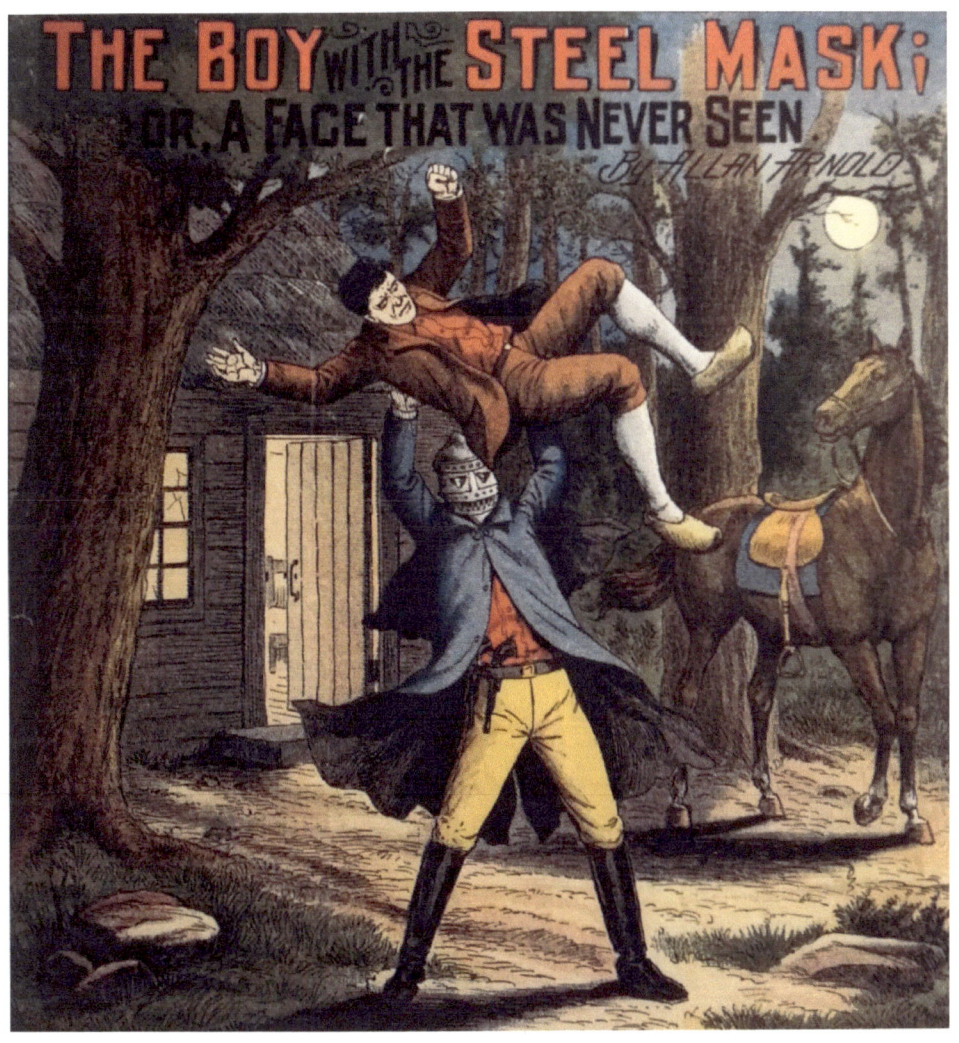

Bowery Boy Weekly No. 92, Bowery Billy's Midsummer Frolic; or, The "Jolly Comrade" Comes to Grief by John R. Conway (house name use by writers including Ernest Avon Young, John H. Whitson and W. Bert Foster).

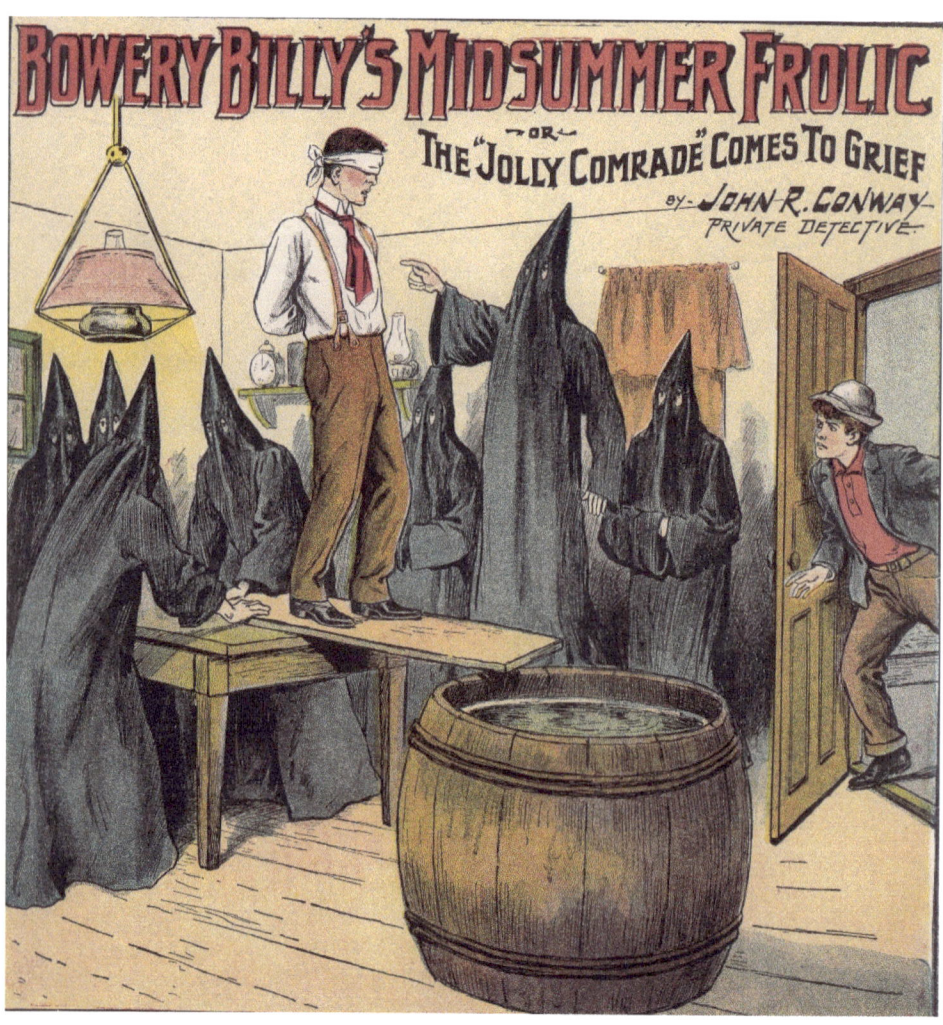

Brave and Bold No. 83, July 13, 1904, The Frozen Head; or, Puzzling the Police by Paul Rand.

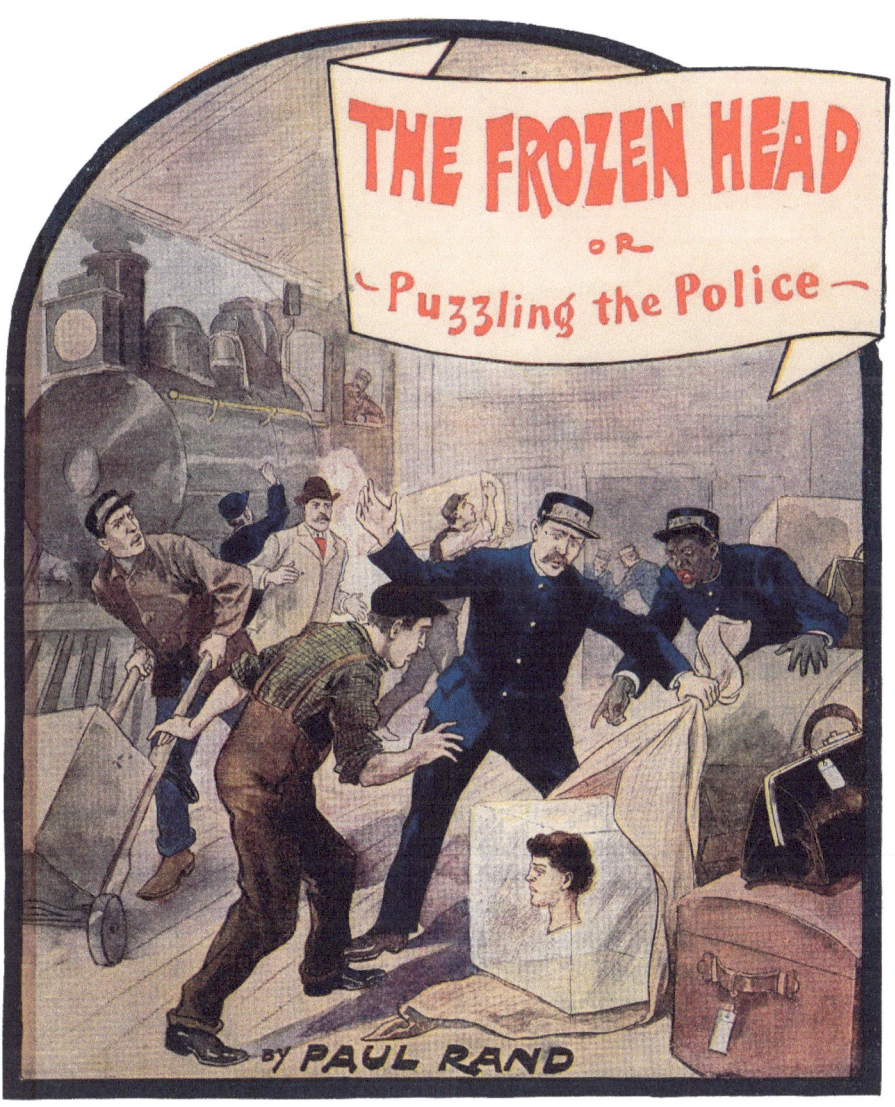

Diamond Dick Jr. Boy's Best Weekly No. 573, October 12, 1907. Diamond Dick Holds the Wire; or, The Mad Lineman of Death Pass by the Author of Diamond Dick".

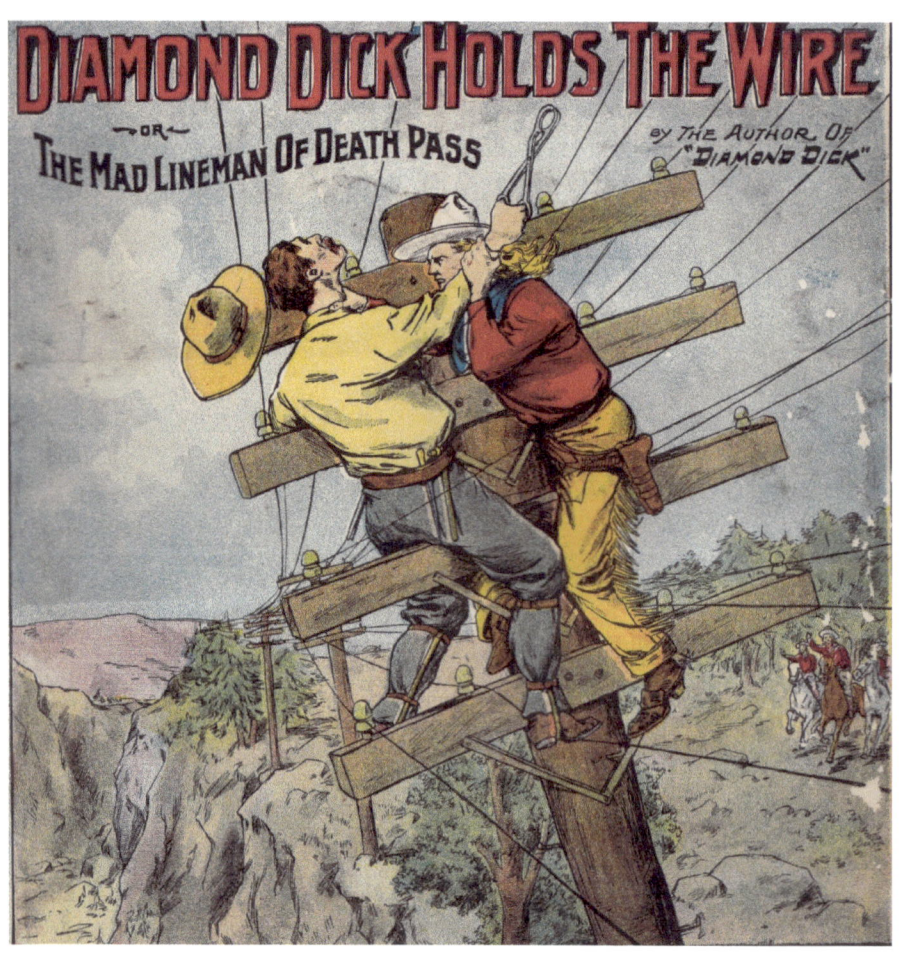

Buffalo Bill Stories No. 468, April 30, 1910. Buffalo Bill's Fiesta Night; or, At Outs with the Baker's Dozen by the Author of Buffalo Bill (house name). Reprinted in France in *Buffalo Bill* No. 245, circa 1930, Une. Nuit de carnaval a Phoenix (One Night at the Phoenix Festival).

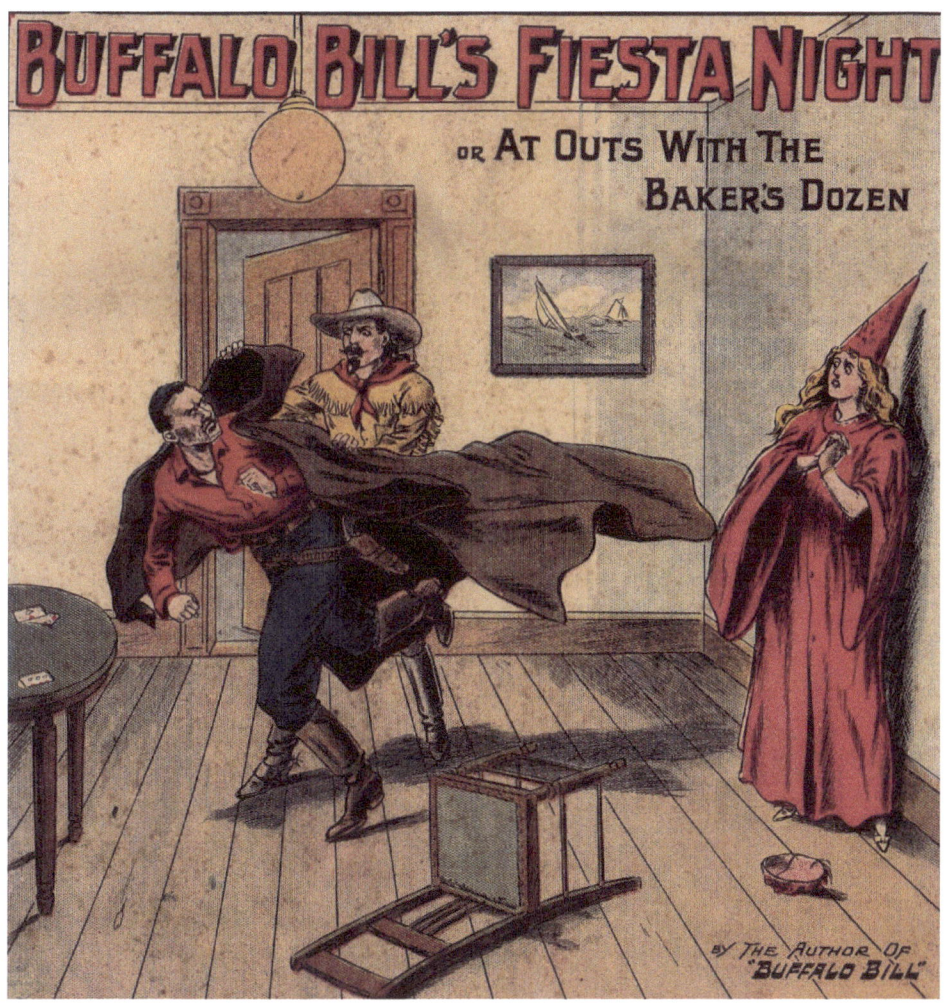

Pluck and Luck No. 139, January 30, 1901. Jack Wright and his Deep Sea Monitor; or, Searching for a Ton of Gold by Noname (Luis Senarens).

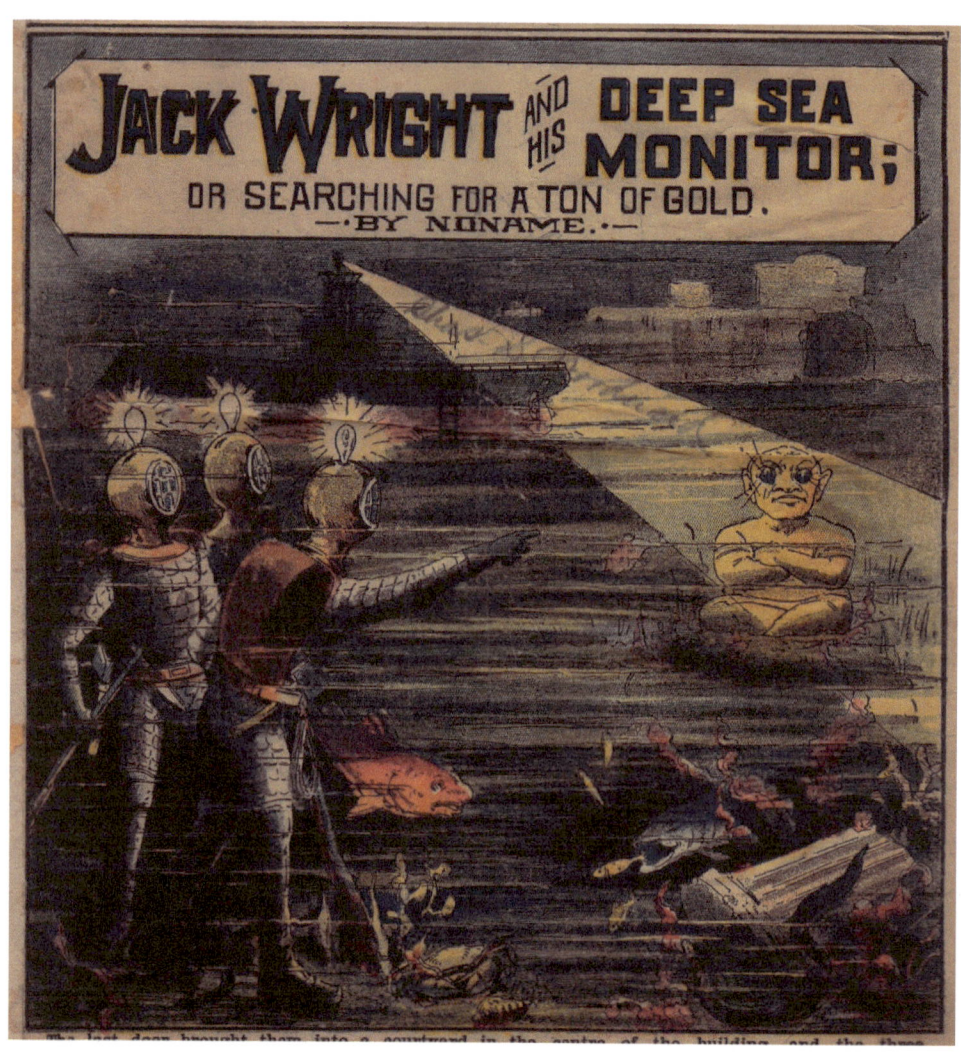

Deadwood Dick Library No. 4, 1899. Buffalo Ben, The Prince of the Pistol; or, Deadwood Dick in Disguise by Edward L. Wheeler. First appeared in *Beadle's Half-Dime Library* No. 28, February 5, 1878, and also reprinted in *Pocket Library* No. 10, March 19, 1884. The third Deadwood Dick story.

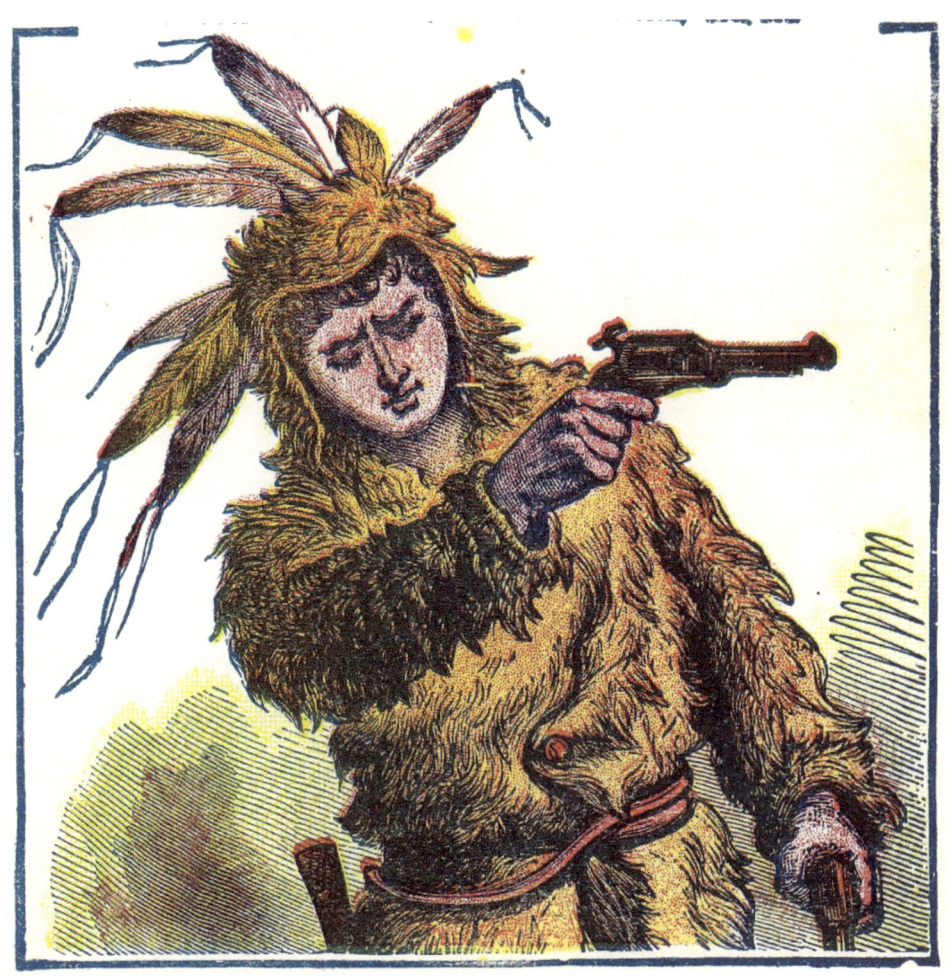

Nick Carter Weekly No. 488, May 5, 1906, A Queen of Inferno; or Nick Carter's Giant Foes by The Author of "Nick Carter" (probably Frederick Van Rensselaer Dey).

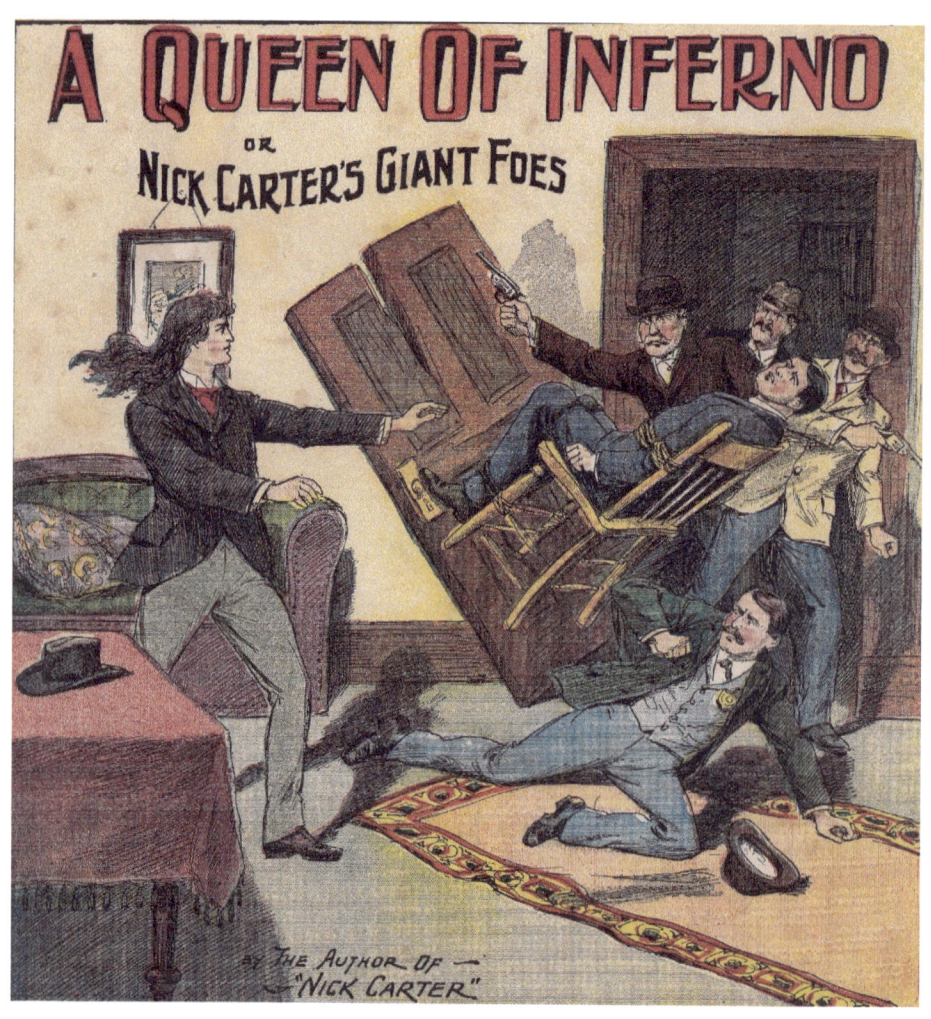

Rough Rider Weekly No. 99, August 25, 1906. King of the Wild West's Chase; or, The Rescue of Yuen Ho by Ned Taylor.

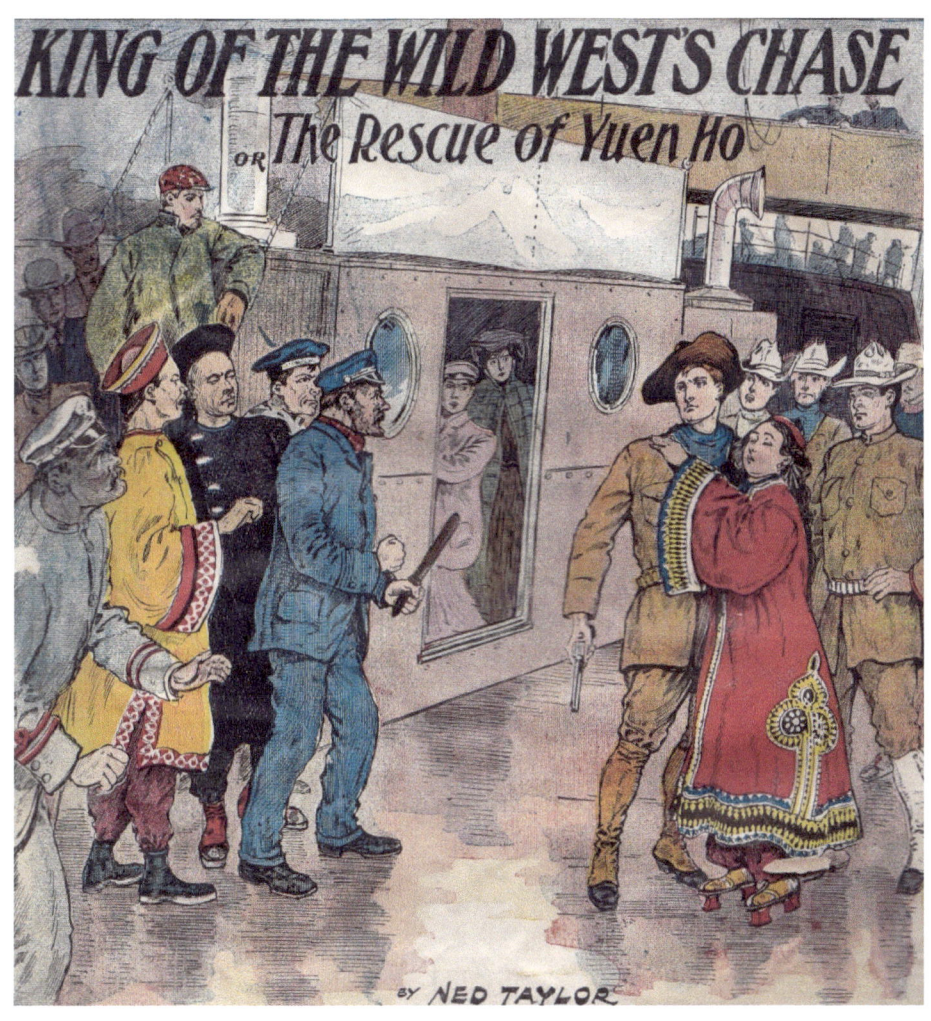

Pluck and Luck No. 497, December 11, 1907. The Seven Tigers of the Mountains; or, All for Love and Glory by Robert R. Montgomery.

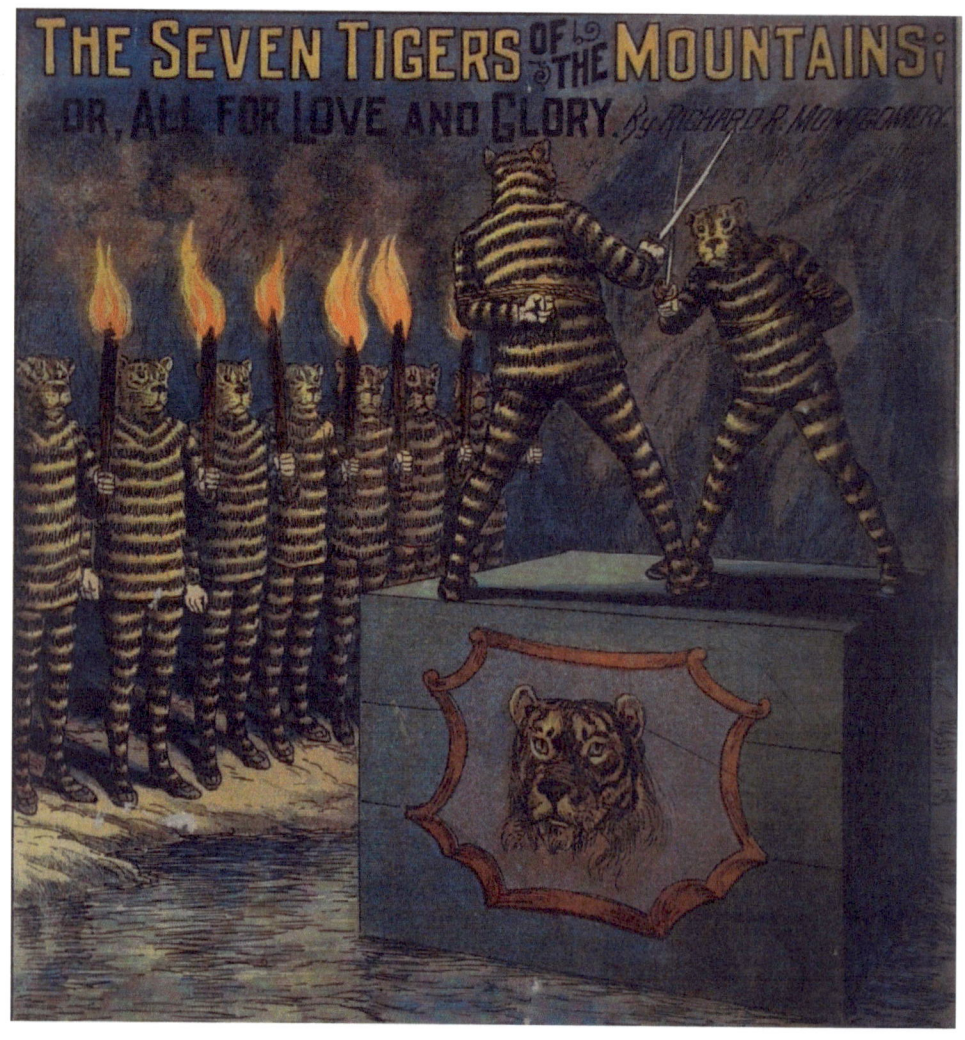

Nick Carter Library No. 224, November 16, 1895.
Patsy's Fight with the Professor; or, The Secret of a
Torn Book by the Author of "Nick Carter."

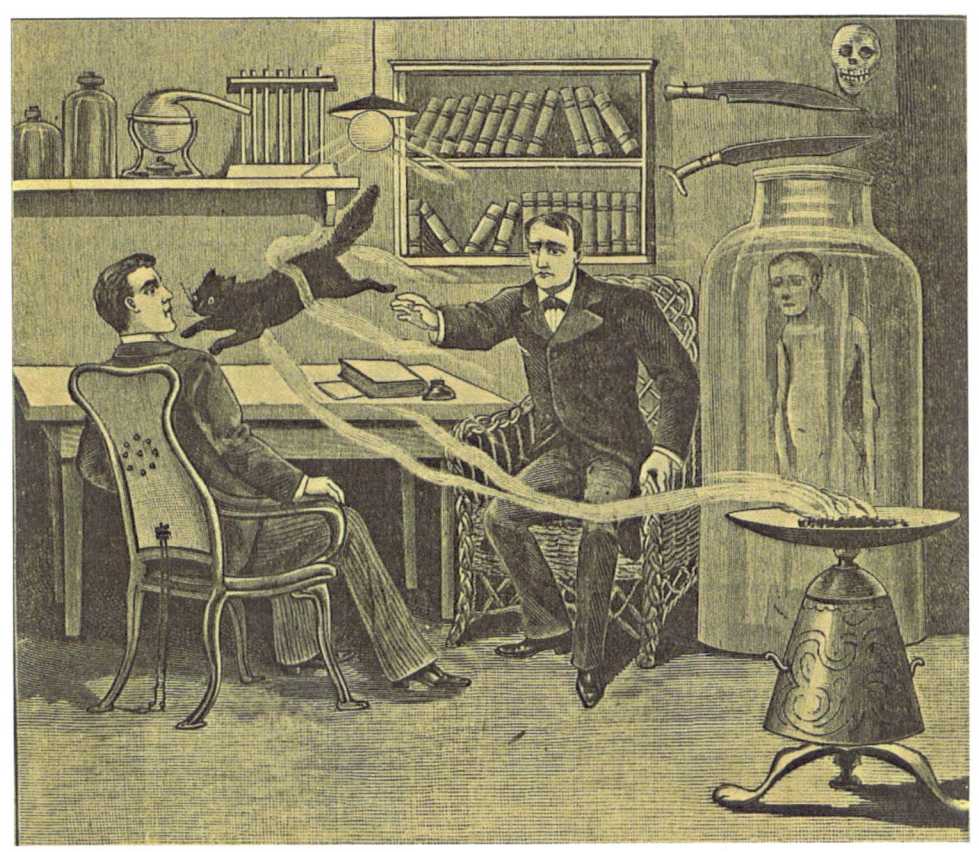

Beadle's Frontier Series No. 11, 1908. Davy Crockett's Boy Hunter by Edward Willett (1830-1899). (Inside title is David Crockett...).

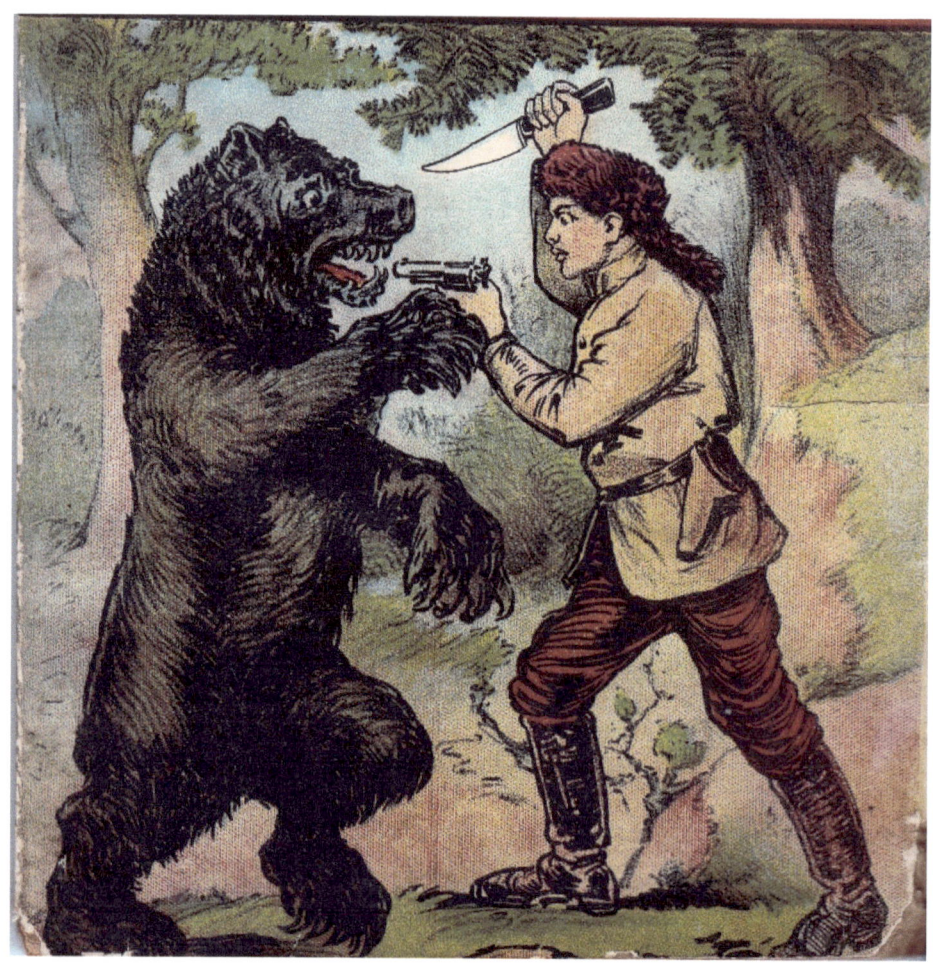

Diamond Dick Jr. Boy's Best Weekly No. 536, September 15, 1906. Diamond Dick in Arizona; or, The Foolhardy Sport of Grand Canyon by the Author of "Deadwood Dick".

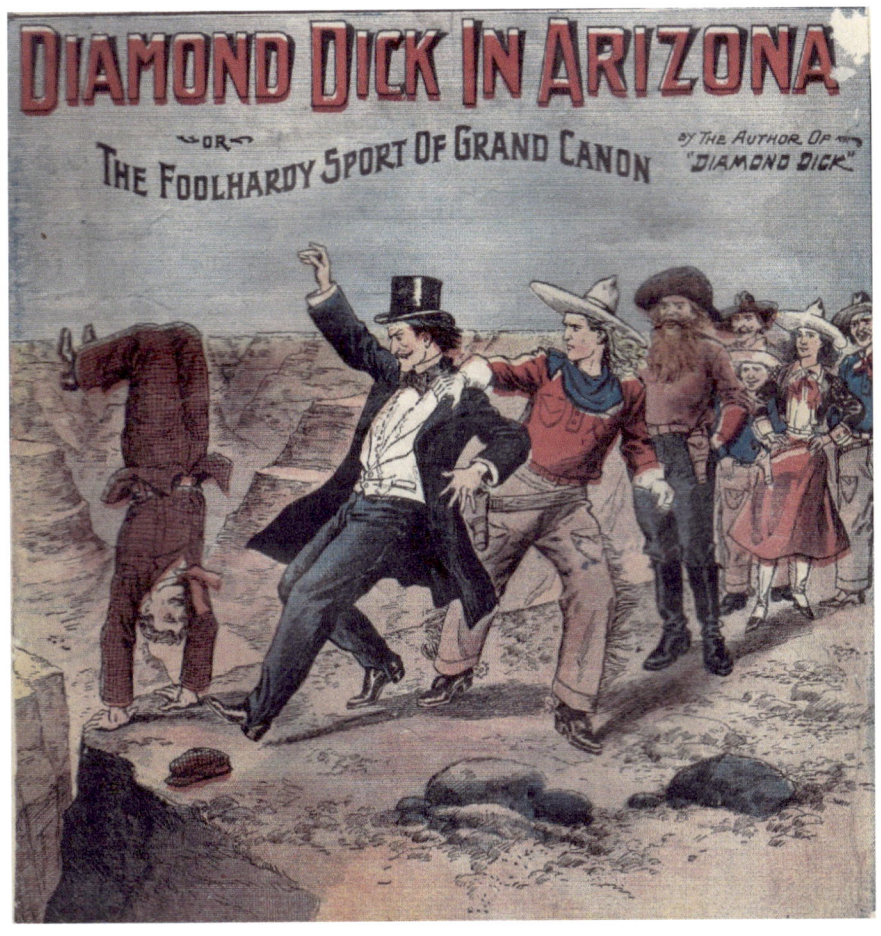

Secret Service Old and Young King Brady, Detectives No. 273, April 15, 1904. The Bradys and the Bond King; or, Working on a Wall Street Case by A New York Detective (Francis Worcester Doughty).

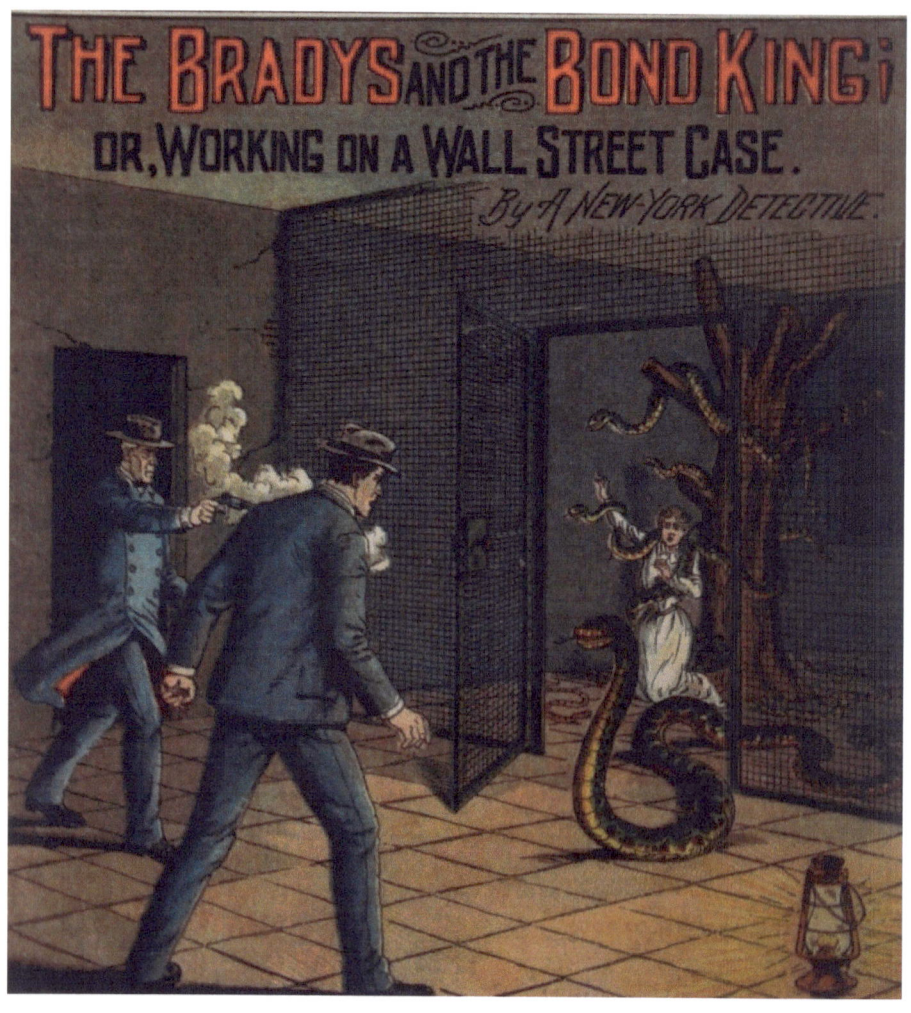

Frank Reade Weekly Magazine No. 39, July 24, 1903. Frank Reade, Jr.'s Clipper of the Prairie; or, Fighting the Apaches in the Southwest by "Noname" (Luis Senarens).

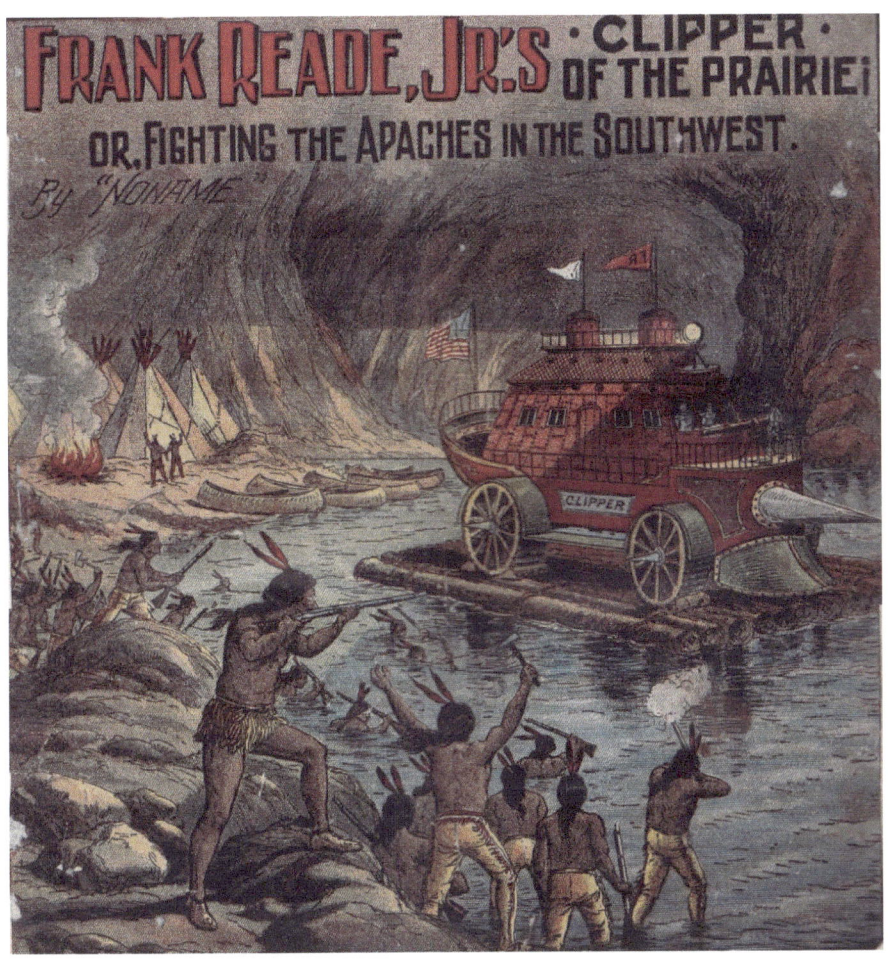

Work and Win No. 905, April 7, 1916, Fred Fearnot's Jubilee; or, New Era's Greatest Day by Hal Standish (H. K. Shackleford).

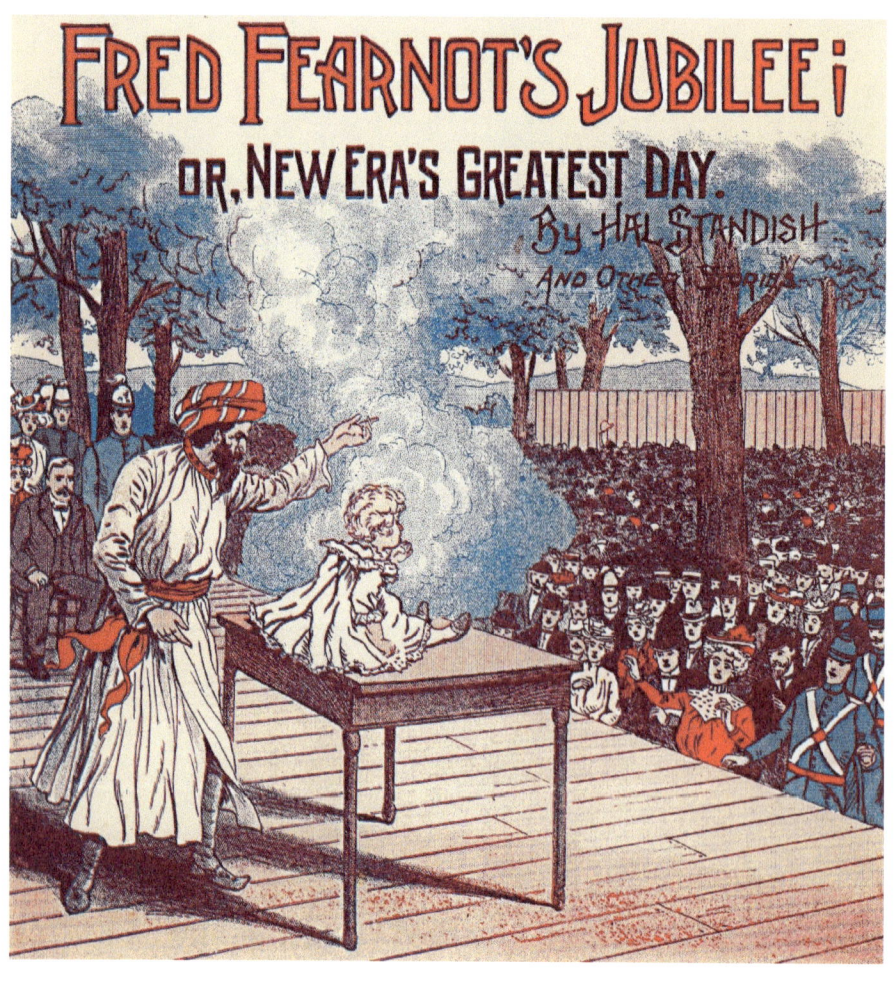

Pluck and Luck No. 910, November 10, 1915. The French Wolves by Allyn Draper (house name). Reprint of No. 96, 1900.

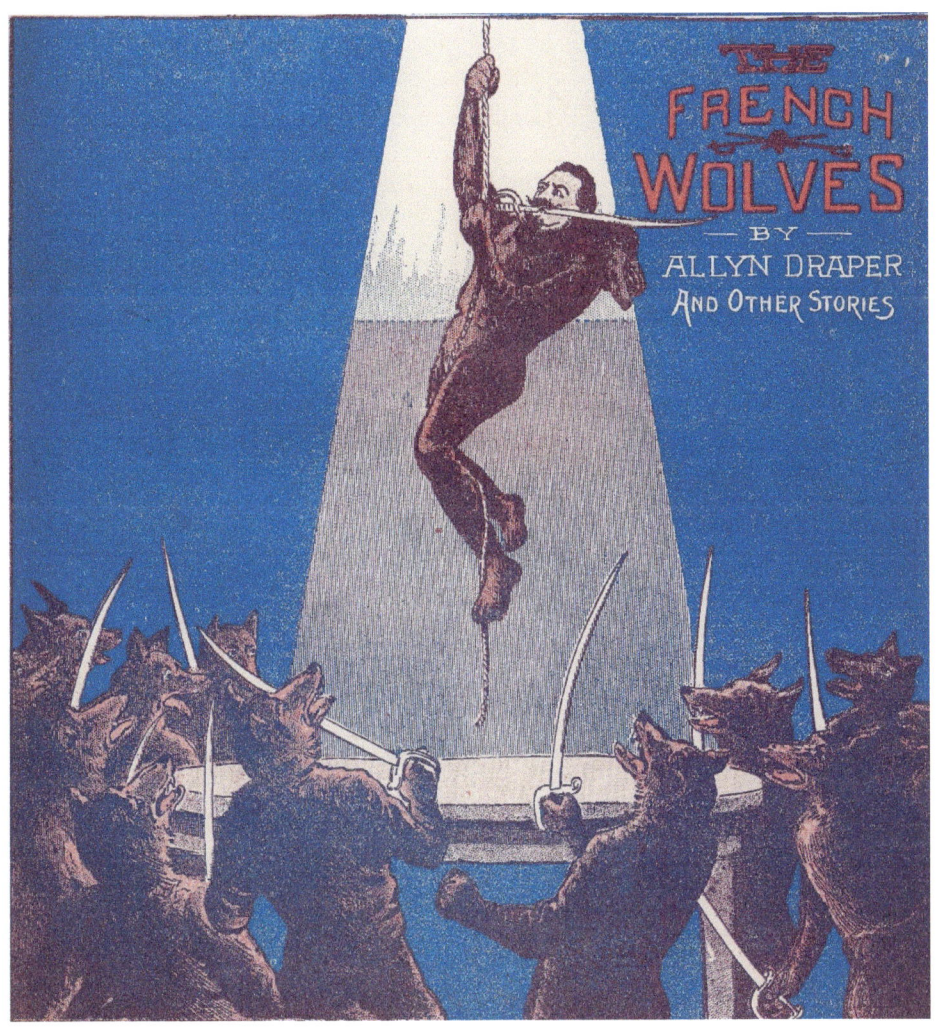

Diamond Dick Jr. Boys Best Weekly No. 593, February 29, 1908. Deadwood Dick's Sure Scent; or, The Marked Man from Chicago. by the author of "Diamond Dick."

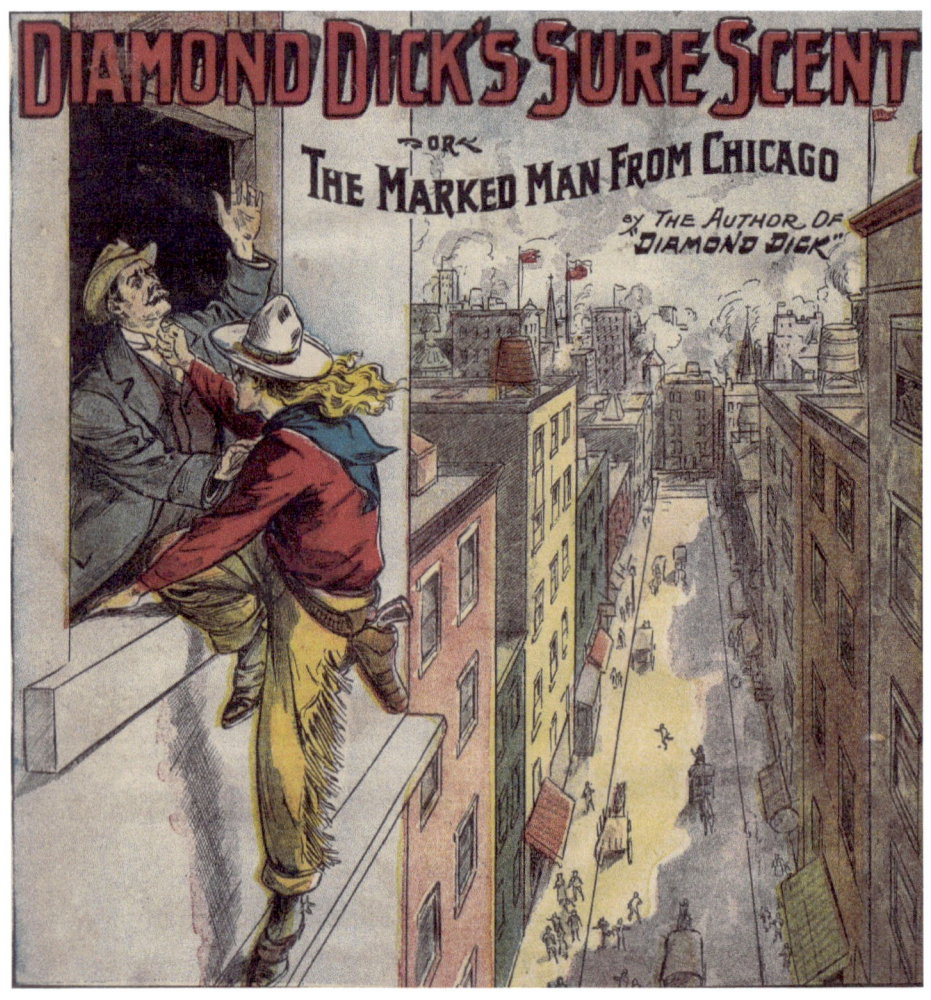

Buffalo Bill Stories No. 335, October 12, 1907.
Buffalo Bill's Ghost Dance; or, the Thrall of
Lightening-That-Strikes by the Author of "Buffalo
Bill."

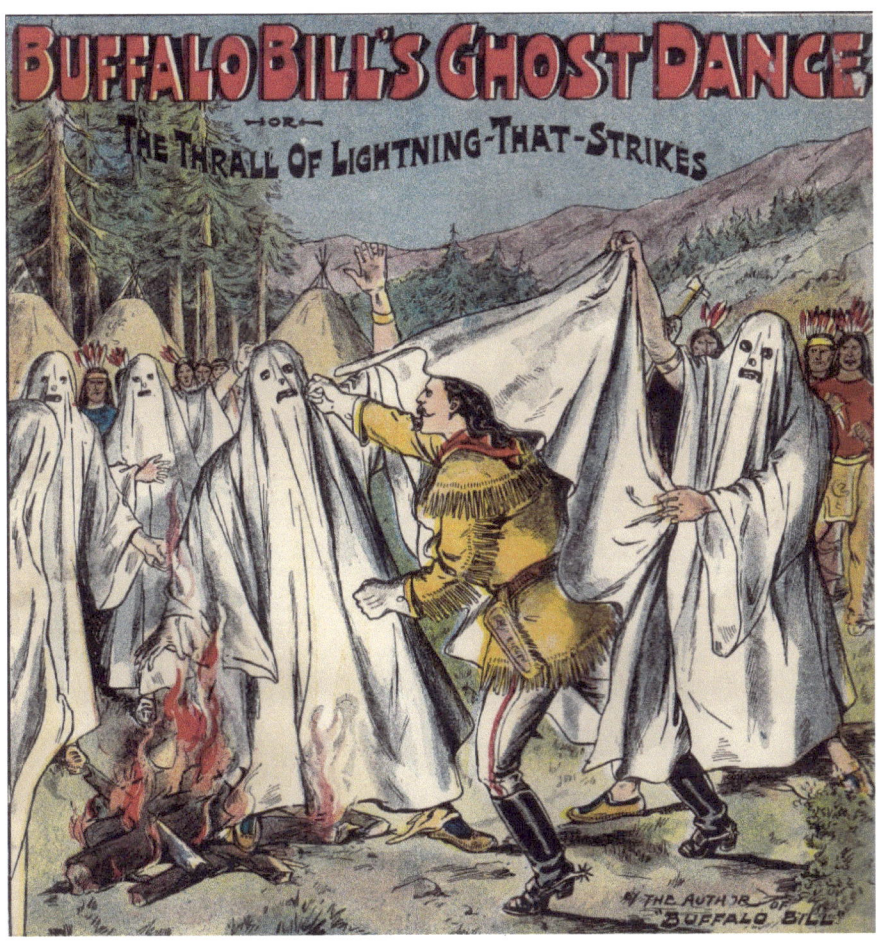

Pluck and Luck No. 1909, October 3, 1917. Jack and I; or, Secrets of King Pharaoh's Caves by Richard R. Montgomery.

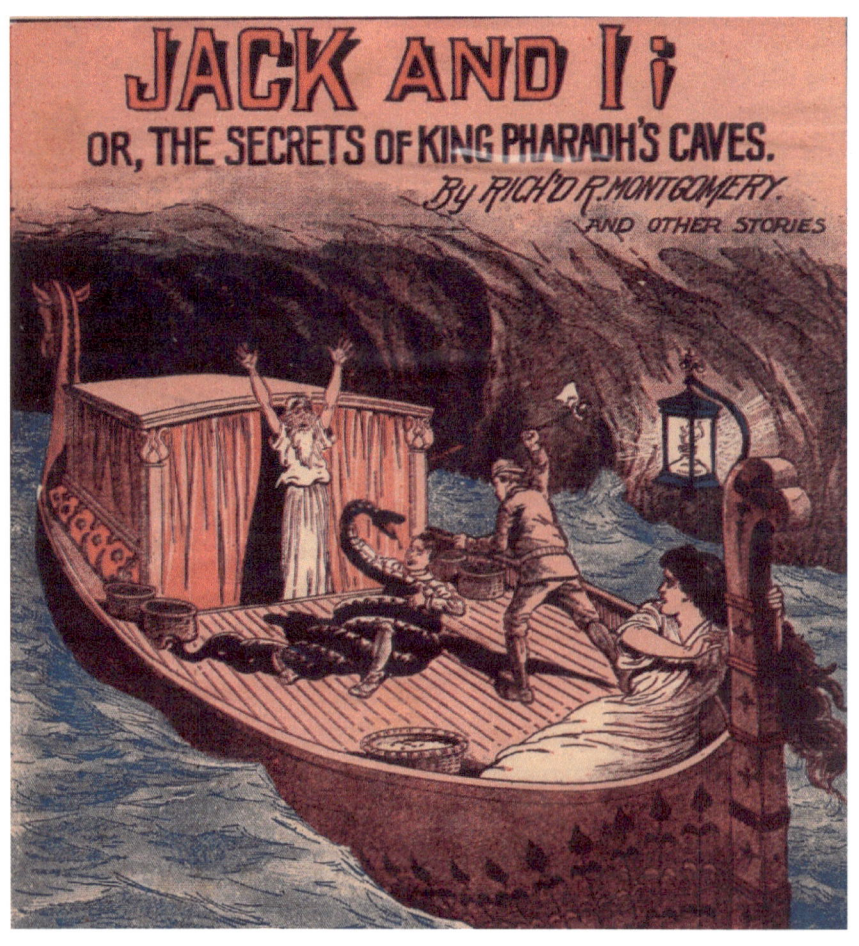

Nick Carter Weekly No. 555, August 17, 1907. "The Mystery of the 7-Up Ranch, or Nick Carter Against the "Brown Chet" Outfit by the Author of "Nick Carter" (Frederick Van Rensselaer Dey).

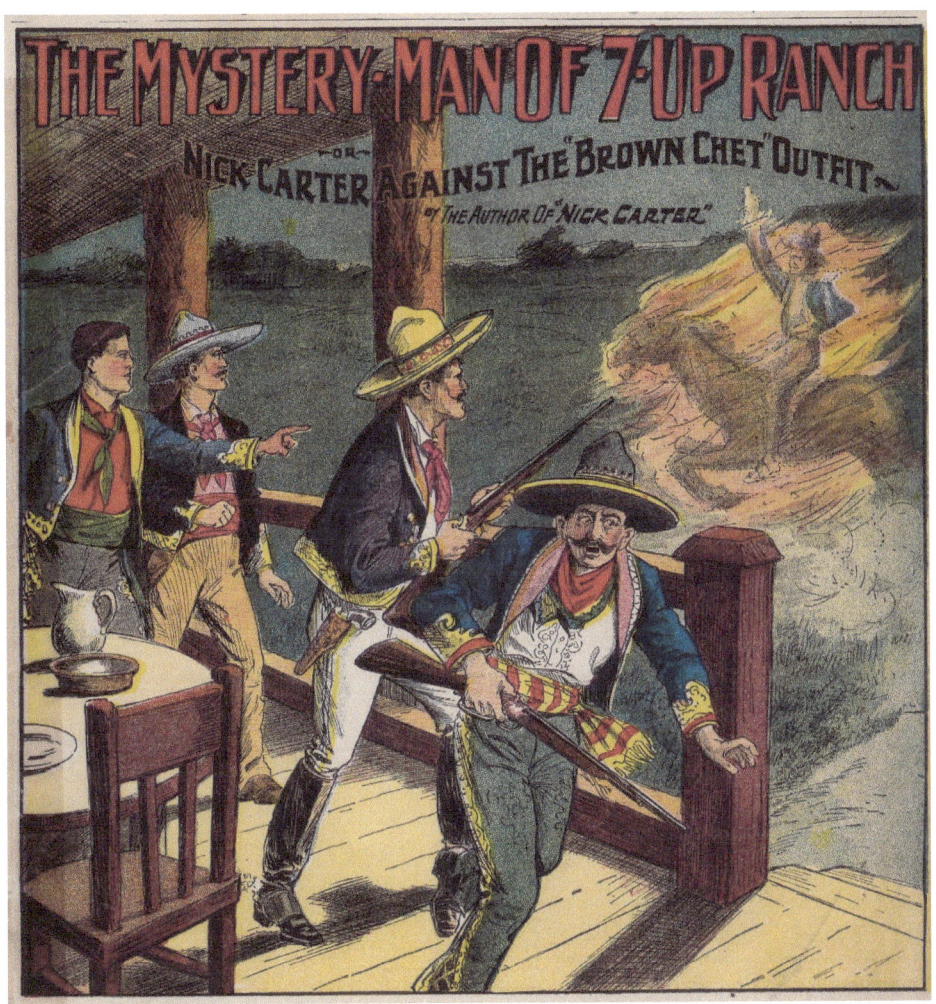

Frank Reade Library No. 81, June 1, 1894. Frank
Reade, Jr.'s New Electric Airship the "Zephyr"; or,
From North to South Around the Globe by "Noname"
(Luis Senarens).

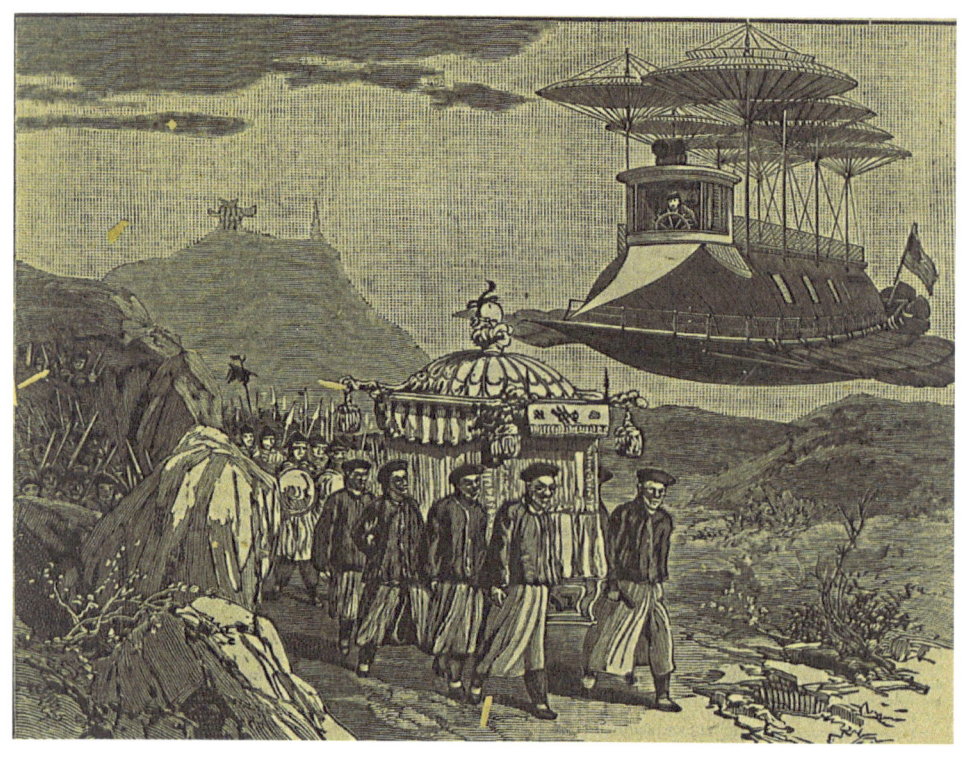

Pluck and Luck No. 195, February 26, 1902. The
Twenty Gray Wolves; or, Fighting a Crafty King by
Howard Austin.

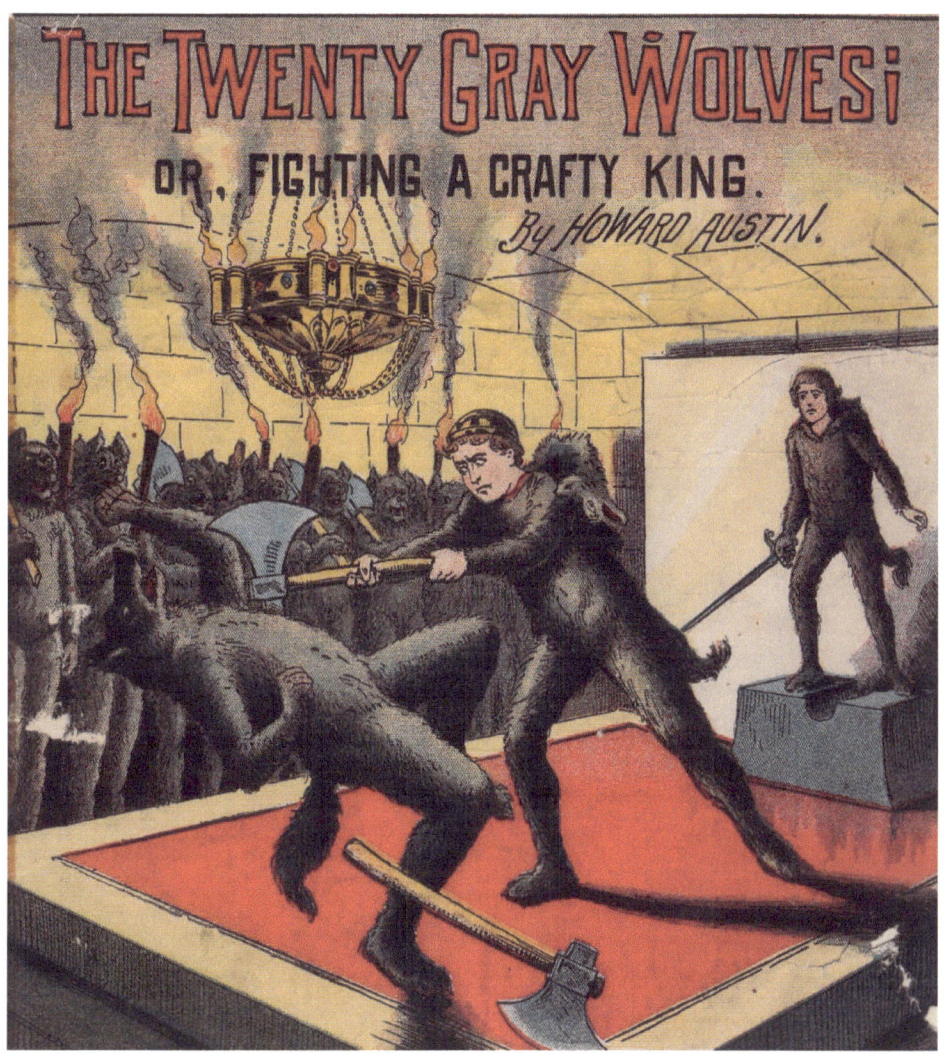

New Nick Carter Weekly No. 666, October 2, 1909, Nick Carter's Master Struggle; or, The Battle with the Man-Monkey edited by Chickering Carter (Frederick Van Rensselaer Dey?).

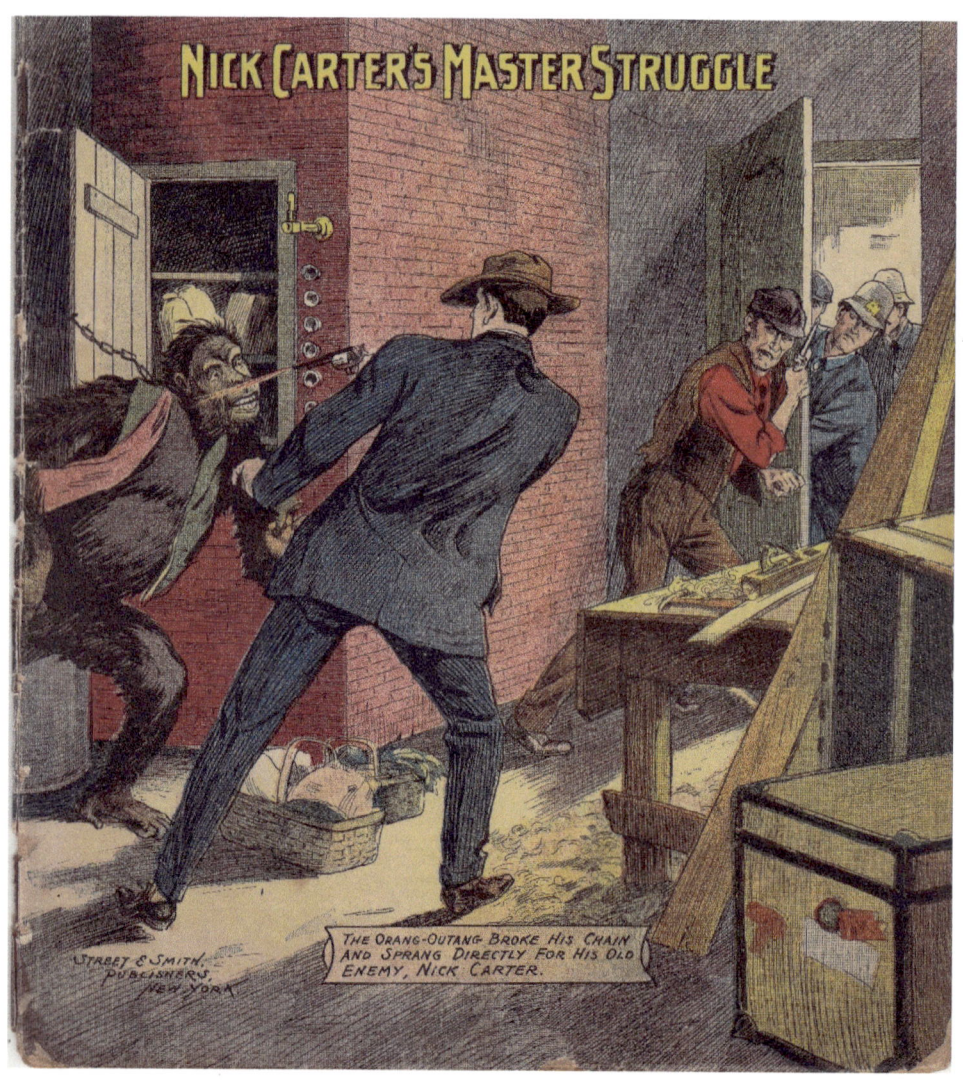

Buffalo Bill Stories No. 324, July 27, 1907. Buffalo Bill's Gold Hunter; or, The Clan of the Skull and Cross Bones by The Author of "Buffalo Bill."

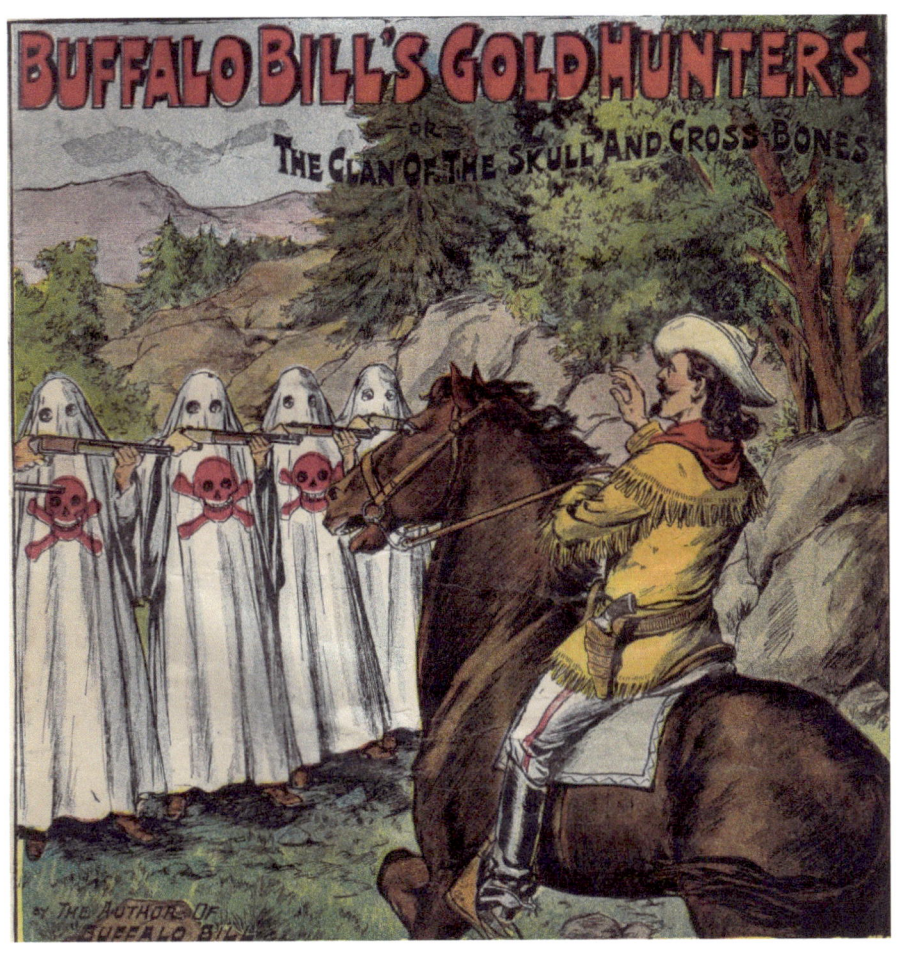

Tip Top Weekly No. 308, March 8, 1902, Frank Merriwell's Discovery; or, The Evil Genius of the School by Burt L. Standish.

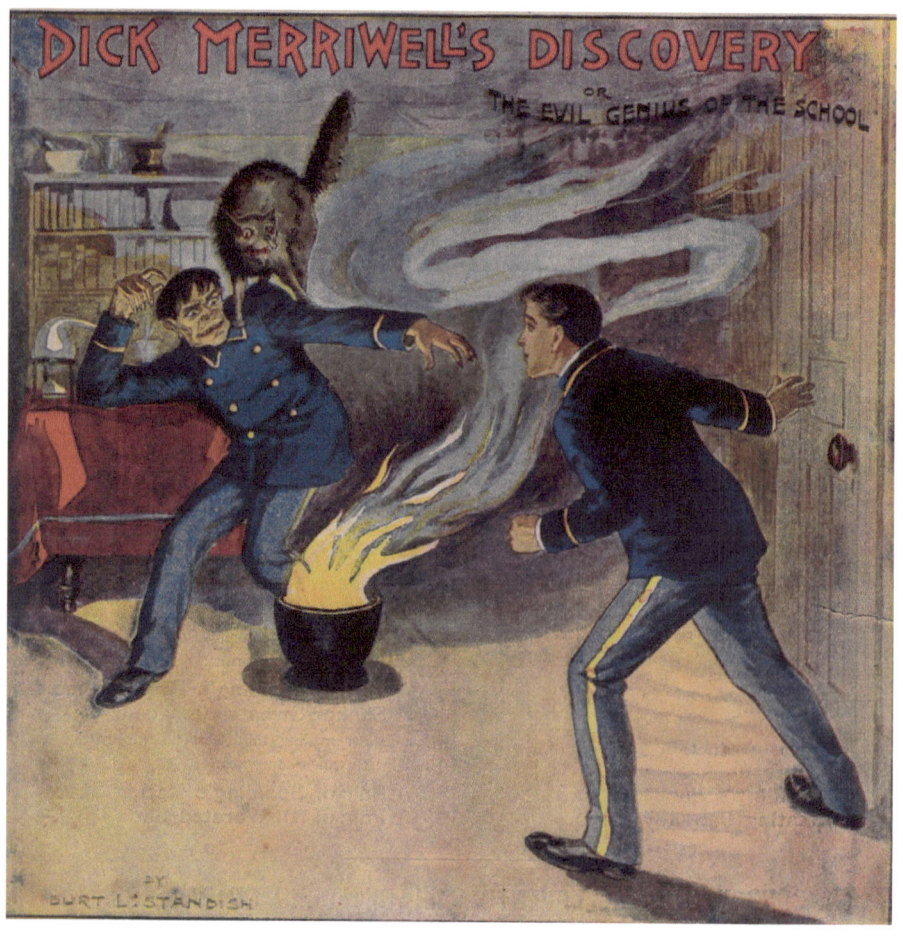

Buffalo Bill Stories No. 210, May 20, 1905. Buffalo Bill's Blind Lead; or, The Treasures of the Comanches by The Author of "Buffalo Bill".

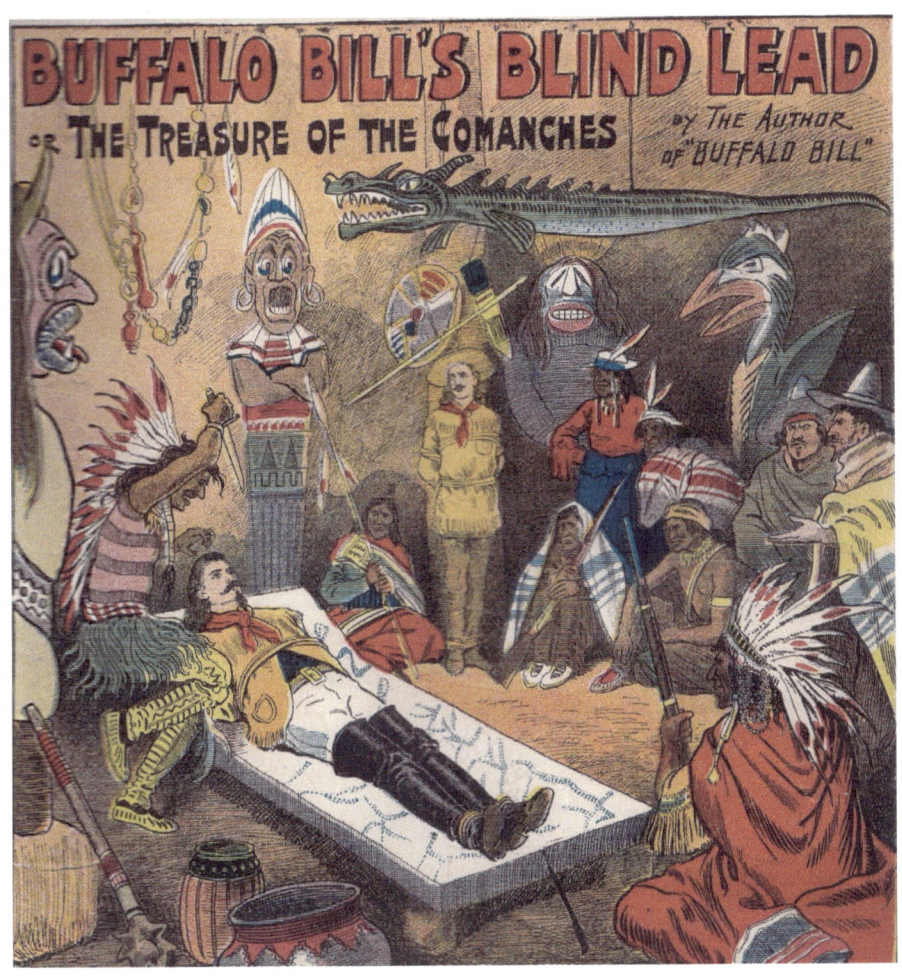

Beadle's Frontier Series No. 17, 1908. Wild Tom of
Wyoming by R.L. Wheeler.

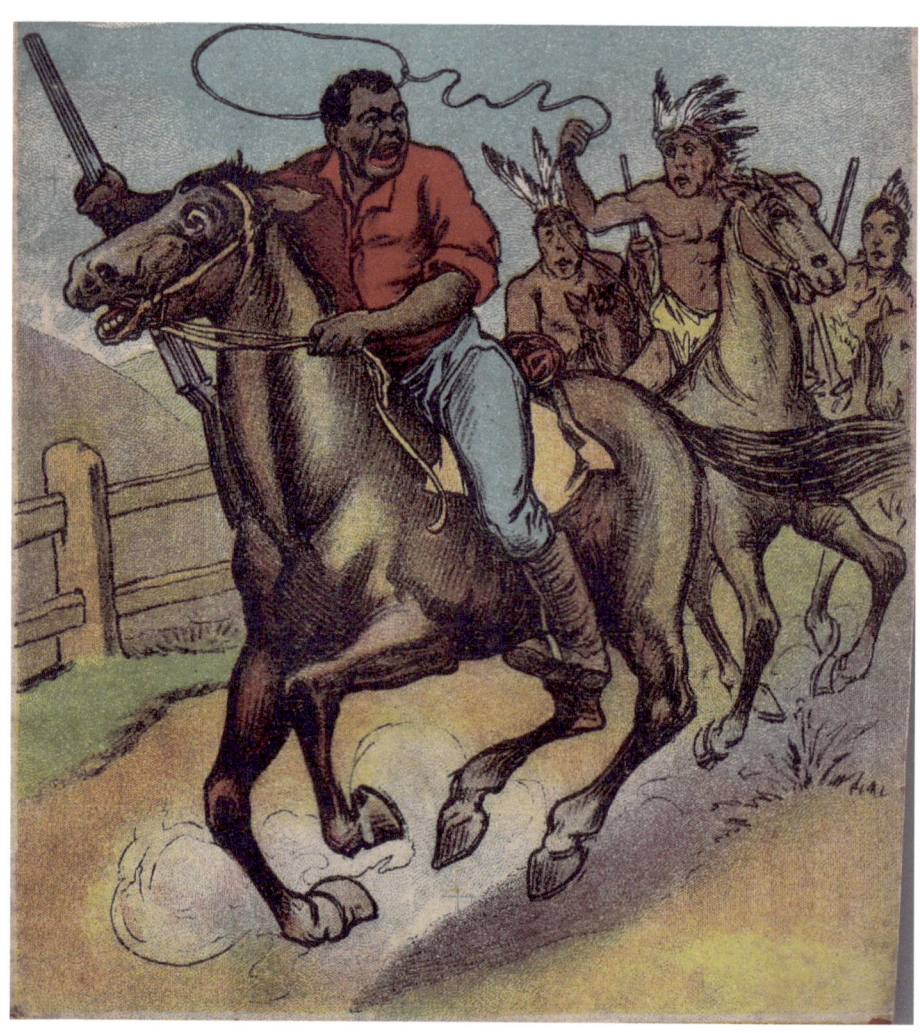

Work and Win No. 245, August 14, 1903. Fred Fearnot's Strange Adventure; or, The Queer Old Man of the Mountain by Hal Standish.

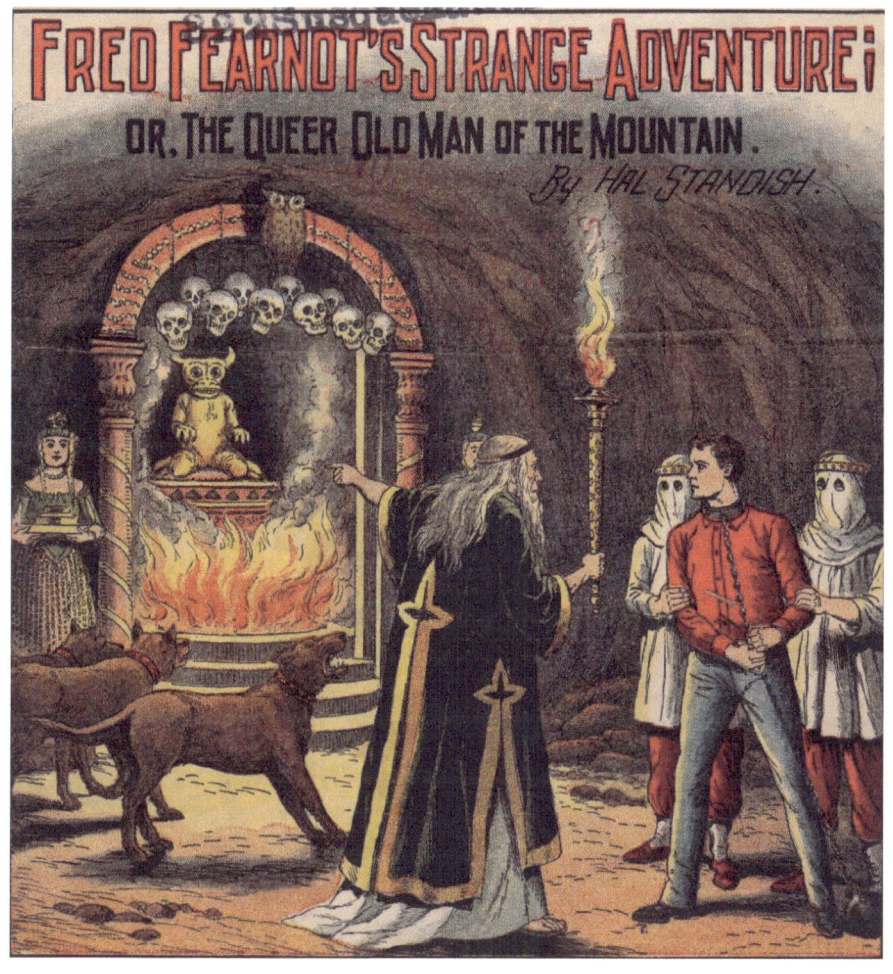

Work and Win No. 942, December 22, 1916. Fred Fearnot and the Hindoo; or, The Wonderful Juggler at Coppertown by Hal Standish (H. K. Shackleford).

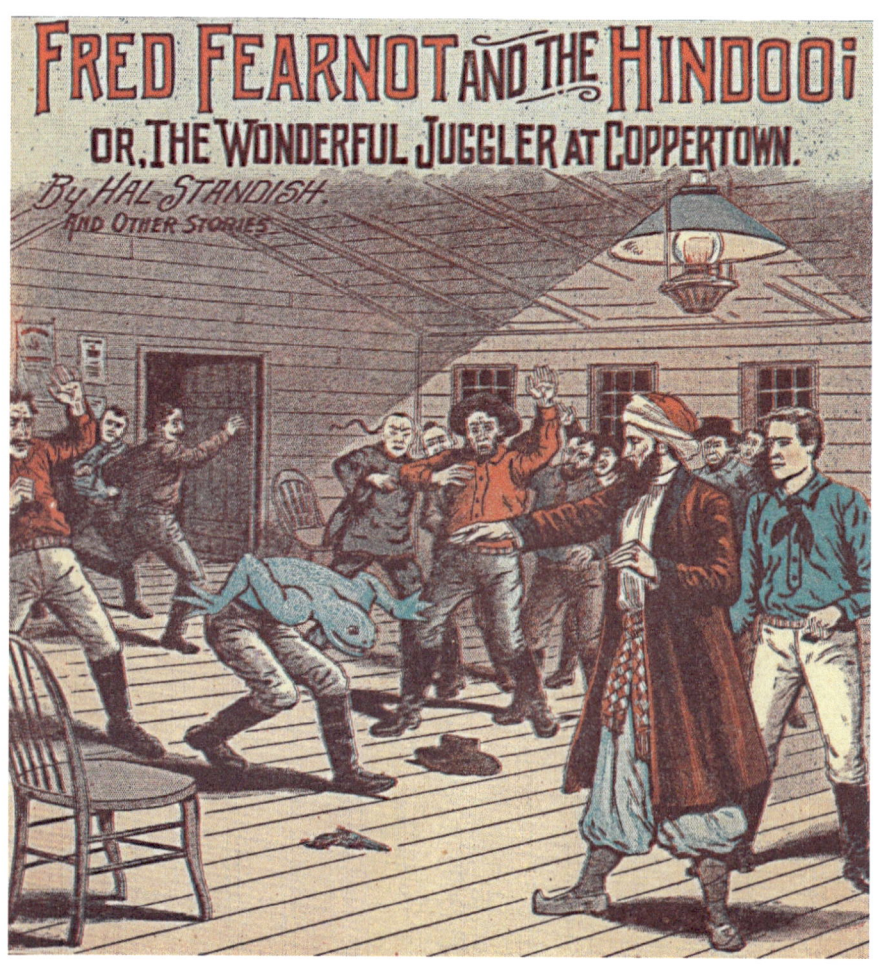

Early Western Life Series No. 13, 1928. Vigilantes of '49 or The Secret Avengers by Texas Pat (Kilpatrick Mason).

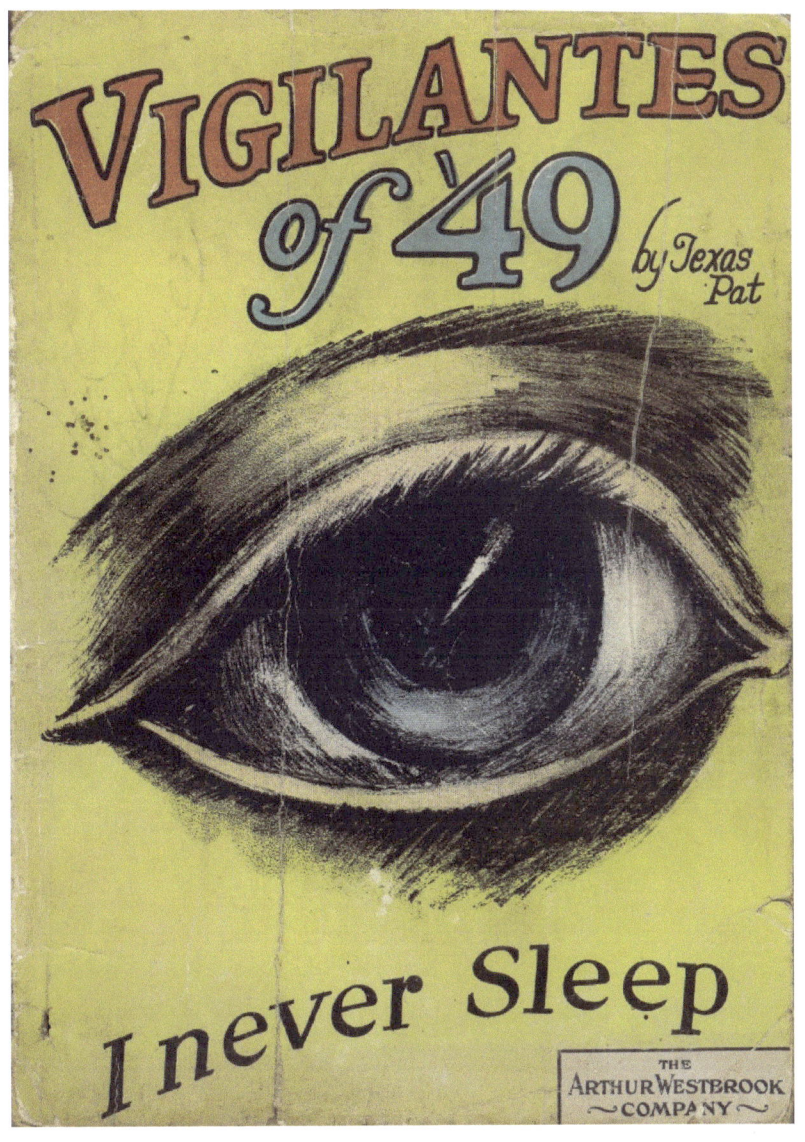

Coming soon:

The Witch Hunter's Wards

Joseph Lovece is a retired journalist and a collector of dime novels, pulp magazines and comic books. He lives in Florida.

www.ingramcontent.com/pod-product-compliance
Lightning Source LLC
Chambersburg PA
CBHW040857180526
45159CB00001B/450